P9-CDS-343

FOLLOWING JESUS

Without Dishonoring Your Parents

Asian American Discipleship

Written by an Asian American team

Jeanette Yep, *coordinator,*
Peter Cha,
Susan Cho Van Riesen,
Greg Jao &
Paul Tokunaga

InterVarsity Press
Downers Grove, Illinois

135/64

InterVarsity Press
P.O. Box 1400, Downers Grove, IL 60515
World Wide Web: www.ivpress.com
E-mail: mail@ivpress.com

Introduction and chapters one, two, three, five, nine and eleven ©1998 by InterVarsity Christian Fellowship/USA. Chapter four ©1998 by Susan Cho Van Riesen. Chapters six and eight ©1998 by Peter Cha and Susan Cho Van Riesen. Chapter seven ©1998 by Peter Cha and InterVarsity Christian Fellowship/USA. Chapter ten ©1998 by Peter Cha.

All rights reserved. No part of this book may be reproduced in any form without written permission from InterVarsity Press.

InterVarsity Press® is the book-publishing division of InterVarsity Christian Fellowship/USA®, a student movement active on campus at hundreds of universities, colleges and schools of nursing in the United States of America, and a member movement of the International Fellowship of Evangelical Students. For information about local and regional activities, write Public Relations Dept., InterVarsity Christian Fellowship/USA, 6400 Schroeder Rd., P.O. Box 7895, Madison, WI 53707-7895.

Scripture quotations, unless otherwise noted, are from the New Revised Standard Version of the Bible, copyright 1989 by the Division of Christian Education of the National Council of the Churches of Christ in the USA. Used by permission. All rights reserved.

ISBN 0-8308-1358-6

Printed in the United States of America ♾

Library of Congress Cataloging-in-Publication Data

Following Jesus without dishonoring your parents / written by an Asian
    American team ; Jeanette Yep, coordinator ; Peter Cha . . . [et al.].
        p.   cm.
    Includes bibliographical references.
    ISBN 0-8308-1358-6 (alk. paper)
    1. Asian Americans—Religious life.   2. Asian American families.
I. Yep, Jeanette.   II. Cha, Peter.
BR563.A82F65   1998
277.3'0829'08995—dc21   97-49194
                                                                           CIP

19	18	17	16	15	14	13	12	11	10	9	8	7	6	5	4	3	2	1
14	13	12	11	10	09	08	07	06	05	04	03	02	01	00	99	98		

To our parents

Introduction: Learning Our Names

Paul Tokunaga

....

ON THAT 1-10 SCALE MANY OF US LIVE BY, WHITE FOLK WERE AL-
ways a 10. I was convinced, as an Asian American, that the highest I
could ever hit was a 7. I grew up in a predominantly white suburb in
the San Francisco Bay area. It was clear to me, even as a child, that
whites set the standards and I had to fit into their society if I was going
to prosper, or even just survive.

In third grade at Hamilton Elementary, two large fifth-grade boys
took me aside. "OK, kid, open your eyes as wide as you can." *Yessir,
two large fifth-grade boys, can do,* I thought. I practiced all the time at
home in front of a mirror. All the "Japanee, Chinee, slant-eye" jabs
from my classmates told me round eyes were much better than my
more angular model. With all the elasticity my eye muscles could
muster, I made like an owl, which sent my fifth-grade antagonists
rolling in their racist laughter.

When we took the standardized tests in sixth grade to determine
how we measured up to the rest of the country, I penciled in my name:
Paul Michael Tokunaga. I proudly admired it. When my mother later
saw it, she did not. She sat me down to write five hundred times: "My
name is Paul Minoru Tokunaga." I was doing all I could to blend in. I
was embarrassed by my Japanese heritage. I wanted to be as white as

I could. White was right. Japanese was not.

The physical comparisons wouldn't let up. No matter how much I yanked on my nose and pinched my wide nostrils, they still wouldn't look like Joe Montana's or Clint Eastwood's. My jet-black hair would not curl unless I slept on it the wrong way, and none of my stretching exercises made me into a six-footer. Of course, the worst came in the high-school locker rooms: why, why, why couldn't I grow hair on my chest like my Italian friends?

Going away to college and having friends who weren't so hung up on appearance, I was able to relax some. But it was clear: if I could choose, I'd pick being white over Japanese any day. Any day.

It took an earth-shaking breakup with a Caucasian woman in college for racial reasons (her mom: "What will the neighbors say? What will your children look like?") to make me face reality: *Paul, you ain't white, you ain't never gonna be white . . . in fact, why do you even wanna be white?* That Damascus Road-like experience forced me to stare at the mirror to see my face and my heritage. God did make me Japanese. Did he goof? Was it a celestial computer error? Was I supposed to be Paul Michael or Paul Minoru?

How Could I Affirm Both as One Person in One Body?
It has not been a smooth road of self-discovery. I have Japanese days and I have American days. Some days I think my Japanese values are the best and American qualities stink to high heaven. Then, when I hear of an Asian American student who is totally stymied by her parents' adamant goals for her life ("Christine, you must be doctor! Must!"), I ache and get angry at the level of control in many Asian American parents. I am very grateful for the freedom to choose our own road that my parents somehow were able to give us children.

At some point in my early twenties, Mom and I were sitting around the kitchen table, working on our fourth cup of coffee, catching up with each other. For some reason, "I'm proud to be Japanese" came out of my mouth.

"What?" was Mom's dumbfounded response. "I thought you were ashamed to be Japanese."

I had to admit that for years I had been, but in recent years I had begun to "own my Japaneseness" . . . and it was growing on me. Later that night, I reflected, *Maybe, just maybe, I can be a 10.*

The Fight for Asian Americans

A couple of decades ago, John White wrote a wonderful book on Christian discipleship called *The Fight.* As our writing team wrestled with the thrust of the present book, we sensed a need for a sort of *The Fight* for young Asian Americans. Discipleship—Asian American style—was what we wanted to address.

In this book we seek to address a large question: "How can I, as an Asian American (primarily college age to thirtyish), follow Jesus with all my heart, mind, soul and strength?" The natural follow-up questions are "What unique qualities about us enhance our ability to love Jesus?" and "What unique qualities or circumstances keep getting in the way of fully giving our lives to him?"

Our aim is to speak to Asian Americans who are somewhere on the journey of discovering they are both Asian and American. Being both means always living with a built-in tension. Those of us who experience less tension than others may celebrate their ethnic heritage. That's great! We hope that reading this book will help you grow in your depth of understanding and obedience. If you are not Asian American, we warmly invite you into this book as a way to get to know us better.

Each chapter addresses what we feel are the major issues we face as Asian American Christians. In each chapter we seek to bring in the insight and authority of God's Word to shed light and bring wisdom from on high.

An interesting phenomenon occurred as we began writing and then reading each others' chapters: our parents kept emerging everywhere! Although we devote two chapters exclusively to relating to our parents, their influence showed up in almost every other issue we addressed. That's because they are so important and integral to who we are. On the one hand, we have tried to honor them. On the other hand, we also want to be truthful about some of the pain we feel from being our parents' children (recognizing, as well, that we have often caused them great pain). We prayerfully hope we have been both loving and honest.

Our book has several shortcomings, and we want our readers to be aware of what they are. We struggled with each of these because we knew they were important and deserved addressing, but space limitations forced us to narrow our focus. We offer our apologies for these shortcomings.

One, we had to limit our writing to the Confucian-based cultures—the Chinese, Japanese and Korean. Our Southeast Asian, Indian, Pakistani and Filipino brothers and sisters face similar issues, but with some different twists and angles. We trust that what we say will ring true and be practical for them.

Two, there is much diversity among Asian Americans that we don't fully address. We don't always distinguish between the Chinese, Japanese and Korean experiences. Clearly there are differences, but again, space and substantial research kept us from addressing the differences. Similarly, immigrant experiences vary widely. What the Ph.D. student from Beijing encounters at a university in the Midwest is distinctly different from the world of the dishwasher immigrating from Guandong to New York City, even though both are Chinese. The histories and cultures of various countries, or regions within countries, are often studies in contrast that we don't attempt to address, knowing that each deserves its own in-depth treatment.

Third, we don't tackle a number of important social and policy issues: racism against Asian Americans, immigrant-related issues, welfare issues and affirmative action, to name a few. We recognize that these are very real issues for Asian American communities.

Finally, we make many absolute statements (Asians are like X, whites are like Y). We know that we are oversimplifying, but we don't have room to discuss the allowances. Look for the truth that the statements contain.

When Generations Clash, Cultures Collide

When Mom wanted me to know beyond any doubt that Minoru was my middle name (I like it a lot now), I suspect she was well aware of how American culture was yanking her children. She didn't want us to deny American culture; she simply wanted us not to give up our

Japanese heritage and culture. She saw value in both.

Philip Slater, in *The Pursuit of Loneliness,* states that America stresses competition, individualism, independence and technology. Asian cultures, on the other hand, tend to stress cooperation, community, interdependence and tradition. "The cultures pull in opposite directions, and it is the soul of the Asian American that provides the rope for the tug of war."

In a doctor of ministry dissertation ("Cultural Pluralism and Ministry Models in the Chinese Community") John Ng quotes John Conner to contrast Asian and Western cultural values.

Asian Value: **Situation Centered**	Western Value: **Individual Centered**
Collectivity	**Individualism**
Group identity	Autonomy
Achievement of goals set by others	Achievement of individual goals
Obligation to group	Trained to be individuals
Duty & Obligation	**Rights & Privilege**
Relational responsibility	Responsible to self
Duty to others	Personal rights
Motivation based on obligation	Motivation based on feelings
Hierarchy	**Equality**
Submissive to authority	Dislike for rules and control
Emphasis on positions in relationships	Play down superiority/inferiority
Accepts rules and propriety	Questions authority
Deference	**Self-Assertion**
Passivity and yieldedness	Aggressive and expressive
Adherence to social politeness	Assertive
Emphasis on self effacement	Open and accessible to others

John Ng, "Cultural Pluralism and Ministry Models in the Chinese Community," D. Min. dissertation, Trinity Evangelical Divinity School, 1985.

Being partly in two worlds but not fully in either makes for a difficult high-wire balancing act. What makes it so tough is that Asian and Western values are often polar opposites. What an Asian American young person experiences at school and in the neighborhood is often in stark contrast to what she or he lives out at home. Pardee Lowe writes the following in the anthology *Growing Up Asian American:*

> For me, at least, it was difficult to be a filial Chinese son and a good American citizen at one and the same time. For many years, I used to wonder why this was so, but I appreciate now it was because I was the eldest son in what was essentially a pioneering family. Father was pioneering with Americanism—and so was I. And more often than not, we blazed entirely different trails.

The Beauty of the East, the Allure of the West

Many of the Western values on Ng's chart affirm personal independence. It wasn't the Asians who coined the phrase "Do your own thing." It wasn't an Asian singer who crooned, "I did it my way." And it certainly wasn't an Asian advertising agency that had its sports mega-superstar assert, "This is my universe."

Such Western values can be very appealing to a young person who has grown up in a culture that submits to authority, puts the group's needs and wants above one's own, and communicates indirectly to avoid offending others.

"Get me out of these chains!" is often the feeling, usually unspoken. The American way looks like a lot more fun. Schizophrenia and tension result when one goes to school and learns how to talk trash, but upon returning home, all one gets to do is silently take it out.

Yet there is an unwillingness to throw the baby out with the bathwater. An appreciation for some of the values exists. Respecting and honoring our parents is a good thing. There is strength in the community that an individual alone can't muster. Yielding to others is biblical. Getting the best education possible has long-range benefits.

What is often missing is the chance to discuss these issues in a way that can bring shared understanding and mutual respect. When both parties go to their rooms and slam the doors, only an uneasy and unsatisfactory détente can exist.

We are both Asian and American. There is beauty and strength in both. The combination of the two cultures can be a terrific blend. As the creator of cultures, God affirms how he made us.

When my self-esteem as an Asian American gets jostled about, I lean heavily on Psalm 139:13-16. Here is my "New Asian American Version":

For it was you who formed my inward parts *[my reflective mind, my deep spirit]*;
> you knit me together in my *[Asian]* mother's womb.

I praise you *[but I don't always lift up my hands]*, for I am fearfully and wonderfully made.

> Wonderful are your works *[even when I stare at the mirror and want to question your choices]*;
>> that I know very well *[I spent a lot of time staring at that mirror!]*.

My frame was not hidden from you,
> when I was being made in secret *[you deliberately chose my Asian features and qualities—I am not a celestial computer error]*,
> intricately woven in the depths of the earth.

Your eyes *[what shape are they, Lord?]* beheld my unformed substance *[that's when you had your chance, Lord, to make me like the others, but you chose to make me unique]*.

In your book were written all the days that were formed for me *[you were choosing the events, friendships, conflicts, the family that would be best for me]*, when none of them as yet existed *[cool]*.

Our lives in Christ, coupled with our heritage as Asian American Christians, are not without purpose. It is certainly no mistake on his part that we were born into our families and cultures, that we live in America and that we are redeemed. Rather than live in denial of any of these three facts, we should be asking, "OK, God, you did this for a reason. How can I best bring you honor and glory?"

May this book do that for you.

1

Pressure, Perfectionism & Performance

....

Paul Tokunaga

"HANDS UP! ALL THE WAY UP! UP AGAINST THE CAR...NOW! YOU'RE under arrest!"

Surely this isn't happening. Japanese Americans are not arrested for stealing. Never.

Crisp fall Friday nights in Northern California are made for high-school football. Tony, Reid and I were to pick up Ron after he finished his shift at the mega-grocery store on Stevens Creek Boulevard, and then head over for the Saratoga-Los Gatos game. A perfect night for four guys without dates. Nothing new for any of us.

The plan had worked the last few Friday nights: just before the nine o'clock closing, several of us pulled up to the rear of the store. This was my first time. We waited for Ron to set a few things out on the loading dock: some cases of beer, a few fifths of vodka, and whatever else looked drinkable. We drove up to the dock, loaded up, pulled around to the front and picked up Ron, who had just punched out for the night. Perfect. We could almost taste that first cold Bud.

This night was different. After we loaded the trunk with the goodies, Tony said, "What's with that guy jogging across the parking lot?" When he veered our way, our curiosity was piqued. When we heard "Hands up! All the way up!" the guessing was over.

Japanese Americans just don't get arrested. As Reid took off for the nearby orchard at the edge of the parking lot, I knew that was on his mind. Reid and I had grown up together since second grade. He lived down the street. He had always been one of my best friends. He was the starting second baseman on the baseball team and the star point guard on the basketball team. We might have broken the law now and then, but getting caught was unthinkable. Facing his parents, who would have to explain his foibles to the Japanese community, was not an option.

The plainclothes officer whipped out his revolver, yelled "Stop!" and then took aim with both hands wrapped around the handle.

Reid ran a zigzag pattern and disappeared into the grove of trees. The officer couldn't draw a bead on him and never fired a shot. He marched Tony and me up to the manager's office, where we met Ron, who had just been fired for his part in our escapade. The officer wanted our quick friend's name.

All of us had watched enough good TV cop shows to know that you never rat on your friends. We were smug and silent, Reid's best friends. At least until they mentioned the F-word.

The thought of being a seventeen-year-old trying to get into college in a few months with a felony on his record did not make my future look too promising. I quickly told him what he wanted to know. Tony and Ron glared at me, but I knew I had just beaten them to the punch.

Amazingly, we were released without being arrested. The agreement was that we had to tell our parents what we had done. No problem: we later decided we would all blame Ron.

Finding Reid that night was fairly easy. He loved to hang out at parking-lot carnivals that had games of chance. There was one about five miles away. He was there when we pulled up.

"You didn't say anything about me, did you? Did you?" Reid was sweaty and jumpy. After Tony and Ron both pointed at me, Reid grabbed me and shook me. I shook back: "Sorry, man, we didn't have any choice!" But I knew exactly what was going through his mind.

His parents, like my parents, had been in the concentration camps for Japanese Americans during World War II. Since being released from camp, they had given themselves to living unblemished, exemplary lives. That meant working hard, sending their children to good colleges and never complaining about the treatment they had received. *We'll show you how wrong you were, American government, imprisoning our families, making us lose almost everything we had worked so hard for. We'll be model citizens. You'll never have an excuse for doing this to us ever again. We'll show you.*

Our parents' silence was deafening to us. Reid and I had lived with the unspoken pressure of being . . . perfect. Do not make waves. Do not bring shame upon the family. Do not be a poor example for your younger brothers and sisters. I, being the eldest son, especially felt that pressure. Sometimes the pressure was too much to bear, as it was for Reid on that Friday night. He had to flee.

The More Recent the Boat Ride, the Stronger the Values
Chinese first came to New York in the 1830s. Asian Indians settled in Salem, Massachusetts, no later than 1851. Japanese arrived in San Francisco in 1869. Filipinos and Koreans came to the U.S. in 1903.

We all grew up with stories passed on to us about the difficulties and sacrifices made in coming to America. Those stories both inspired and intimidated us. We were proud of what our forebears had done to make it possible for us to live in this great country of opportunity. We were also fearful: What if I blow it? What if I let my father down? His father? His father's father?

We grew up with strongly instilled values. Within Asian cultures is a strong emphasis on honoring the family. Getting the best education possible was highly valued. Being successful meant having a position in a few select fields, such as medicine, engineering or business. We would take care of our elders.

I recently met with a pastor of a Chinese church on the East Coast. The congregation is largely made up of immigrants and their children, who range from toddlers to young adults. He told me, "The church elders have made it very clear that 'we are a Chinese church, not Chinese American. Our identity is as Chinese only.'"

On paper this might look fine, even admirable, for there is much to be admired about Chinese ways. But when a Chinese couple's young child sits in class with Caucasians, African Americans and Hispanic Americans—all of whose roots in this country go back several hundred years—there is a clash. East meets West. I cringe for that church as the young Chinese Americans are being jerked one way and then the other.

With most Asian nationalities, the closer to the immigrant experience, the stronger the pull to retain the values of the homeland. Each homeland, whether it is China, Taiwan, Japan or Korea, is different and brings its unique values and pressures to the situation. In one sense there are no Asian Americans, all looking, dressing, thinking and eating alike. There are just Chinese Americans, Japanese Americans and Korean Americans.

The first generation willingly plows the hard soil of the immigrant life in order to help their children achieve the American dream of success and plenty. They won't do it, however, at the expense of their culture.

The evolution is seen most sharply in the second and third generations: English becomes the dominant language at home, the children begin dating outside their culture, and they are thinking American. By the third generation, says Joann Faung Jean Lee in *Asian Americans,* "Asian Americans will have developed values inherently Western. This is in part because of the strong desire to do well in American society and an emphasis on education. The vocabulary of success is defined in Western terms: from language to cultural symbols."

The Confusion over Being Confucian

All immigrants face uphill challenges and have dreams for a better life than back in the "old country"—if not for them, then for their children and their children's children. Unique to Japanese, Chinese and Korean immigrants, however, is the influence of Confucius.

Confucius (K'ung Ch'iu) was a Chinese philosopher who lived from 551 to 479 B.C. In the midst of social upheaval, he tried to bring social and civic order. It is unclear if he ever put anything in writing, but his small band of followers compiled his teachings into the *Analects.*

The tenets of Confucianism center around the concepts of *jen* and *li*. *Jen* is a combination of the characters for "human being" and for "two"; thus, empathic humanity should be at the foundation of human relations. *Li* is a combination of morality and etiquette, custom and ritual.

Also at the heart of his teaching was the concept that successful individual human relations form the basis of society. To bring order to society, one must first bring order to the family. Order in the family ultimately brings order to the community, which brings order to the government.

Some other strong values of Confucianism include parental authority and honor (known as "filial piety": children must honor and obey parents, putting their parents' comfort, interest and wishes above their own), social hierarchy, male dominance, duty and obligation.

If we look at John Conner's chart (p. 13) showing the differences between Asian and Western values, we see that Confucius's teachings have clearly influenced Asian values. When Confucianism and rugged Western individualism show up in an Asian American home, sparks are going to fly. On Conner's chart, especially with today's emphasis on family values, the Asian value side looks quite appealing. That's because there is good in aspects of Confucian thought. There are some values that are very compatible with Christianity.

Like Confucianism, the Bible calls us to honor our parents (Leviticus 19:2-3; Deuteronomy 5:16; Proverbs 6:20-23; Ephesians 6:1).

Like Confucianism, we are called by God to put the desires of others above our own (1 Corinthians 10:24; Philippians 2:3-4).

Like Confucianism, Christianity recognizes that when primary relationships (such as those within the nuclear family) are made right, the larger society is bettered.

But there are aspects of Confucian thought that clash with Christian faith. Some of it may be because of differing missions, some of it because of differing ideology.

Confucius was attempting to set down rules for a stable and orderly society for the entire country. He was speaking to a chaotic social situation. The message of Jesus, on the other hand, was for his "new society" of followers, who would live out their faith in the midst of an unbelieving world. He was not setting up a "new world order" for all.

Confucius's rules were highly male-oriented. The mother's side of the family had little importance. Daughters or wives did not inherit wealth. The wife joined the husband's family and identified wholly on that side, with minimal ties to her family. Jesus was certainly more egalitarian and gave more prominence and recognition to women.

Although Jesus gave honor to family, he always gave greater honor and favor to the "new family," his body. In Confucianism duty and obligation to the family always come first. For Confucius, the two most important relationships within the family are those between father and son and between the oldest and youngest brothers.

When it came to eternal life, Jesus often spoke of it. Confucius offered no hope of life after death.

For most Asian Americans, Confucianism is not a religion or even a philosophy to which they would intentionally devote themselves. Rather, it permeates the social and family structures, much in the way Americans do not recite the Declaration of Independence but certainly have the values of the Declaration woven into the fabric of their society.

> ### The Equation That Causes Heart Abrasion (or Ingredients for a Potion That Causes a Huge Commotion)
>
> Ingredients:
> 1 part Confucian thought
> 1 part Western thought
> 1 part incredibly high parental standards
> 1 part Model Minority
> Toss into an unbreakable mixing bowl. With a blender, mix at high speed for about 20 years. Makes 1 large serving of Driven, Perfectionistic, Schizophrenic Young Person. Best served with side dish of kimchee, sushi or jiao zi. Caution: sweet first bite may be followed by bitter aftertaste.

Feeling Pressure from Our Parents

Whenever I talk with Asian American students and young adults, it doesn't take more than a few minutes before they are sharing deeply about their parents. When I talk with non-Asian American young people, we'll sometimes talk about their parents, but only after I probe a little. What usually surfaces are concerns for their parents' marriage, job relocation or getting help from home for tuition. Conversations with Asian Americans are much different. For them four pressure points seem to keep surfacing.

First and primary is the importance of a good education. Again, the closer to the immigrant experience one is, the greater the pressure one feels.

"A first thing to understand is the incredible pressure first-generation Asian American students feel behind them as they enter college," writes Ray Lou, professor and director of Asian American studies at San Jose State University. "Immigrant or refugee parents leave native homes at great personal risk 'so our children can attend an American university.' Their children feel strong needs to 'show gratitude' for those struggles: 'I want to do well in school to honor my parents. I want to get a good-paying job to help my family. It is the least I can do'" ("Model Minority? Getting Behind the Veil," *Change* 7 [November/December 1989]).

A second pressure point for many Asian Americans is that we remain children until we marry. In practice this means that whereas our Caucasian friends are making adult-type decisions at twenty-one (some even at eighteen), our parents continue to see us as children.

As they graduate from college, our Caucasian friends are making their own career decisions, selecting their spouses, choosing where they will live and buying their own cars. Many of these major choices are made on their own with little or no input from their parents. Not so with Asian Americans.

The goal of Asian American parents is admirable. A strong theme of their lives is to provide well for their children. The Japanese have a saying, *Kodomo ni tame ni*—"for the sake of the children." They work extremely hard in order to provide well for their children and to allow them to receive the finest education possible. Often they feel that their job is not complete until their child marries, which is when they finally are released from the responsibility.

In Western culture, the aim of parenting is to launch children so that they gradually make it on their own. Little by little, parents give increasing freedom to the child, like letting out rope. Within Asian cultures there is much less of a transitional phase. The adolescent and young adult phases are deemphasized. When we marry, we move from childhood to adulthood in a swift leap.

During the past several years, I have had numerous conversations with Asian American college students and young professionals about these issues. I'll never forget meeting with a premed student from Denver.

I was speaking at a Korean American conference outside of Denver. During a talk on figuring out career choices, this student politely interrupted me.

"All of what you are saying sounds good . . . but it doesn't really apply to me. You see, my parents only gave me three options. I could become a doctor, an engineer or a businesswoman, as long as I was a highly successful one. You talk about offering my career options to God. Well, I can't. I can only offer one of these three to my parents." As she finished, the room filled with nods of agreement.

A few months later, at a Korean American conference in Philadelphia, I related that story. A student proudly replied, "Oh, parents back here are much more open-minded. We get a fourth choice. We can be lawyers, too."

Recently I met with Steven, a second-generation Chinese American on the West Coast. He had graduated from one of the premier engineering programs in the country and was working for a consulting firm. While the job was "OK," as he put it, his heart was clearly elsewhere. He loved working with the youth at his church. He headed up the youth basketball program. He was there at just about every youth activity the church sponsored. The kids flocked to Steven like he was the Pied Piper. They hung on every word. When Steven described his youth work, he lit up like a Christmas tree. It was clearly his passion.

His church had been actively searching for a youth director for well over a year, but without success. "Steven, you're not happy with your job. Why don't you apply? You'd be great at it!"

His face dropped and his eyes never left the floor. "My parents would never let me. They would never let me leave engineering."

The irony? Steven's parents are cornerstone leaders in the church. They love the church, they are praying for a great youth director, but they could not consider their own son being a candidate. Steven is a young adult professional, lives on his own and has a well-paying job, but clearly he is still a child in his parents' eyes.

A third pressure point from our parents is marrying the right person.

When I was in high school, Mom once said to me, "If any of you marry a hakujin (Caucasian), don't bother to come home." A few years later, when I was a junior in college and dating a Caucasian fairly seriously, Mom said, "If you marry a hakujin, I will . . . love . . . her. It won't be easy, but I will love her."

I was deeply moved by Mom's change of heart. She knew it would take hard work, as she had been severely and rightly scarred by the internment of World War II, which was done, in her eyes, by a "white American government." Mom has proven true to her promise. She has loved my wife, Margaret, a hakujin from Mississippi (yes, Mississippi!), like her own daughter these past twenty years.

One funny story: After Margaret and I began dating seriously, I thought I needed to prepare my parents for a possible engagement. I was living in Wisconsin, Margaret in Atlanta, and my parents in California.

"Mom, I'm getting serious with a young woman, Margaret. She was born in Texas and raised in Mississippi. She lives in Atlanta. And . . . she's a hakujin." (Not that Mom could picture a Japanese living in the South, anyway.)

A long pause.

"Does she have the accent—and the whole thing?"

In my desire to best prepare Mom, I couldn't help myself, "Mom . . . the whole thing!"

"Oh . . ."

Mom and Dad have been incredible, unconditional troopers in loving their daughter-in-law and their grandson, Sam, who is hapa (half Japanese, half other). But not all Asian American parents share their attitude.

The spectrum of parents' attitudes on whom their children marry usually looks like this:

Only marry within our nationality.	It's not OK to marry outside our nationality.	I guess it's OK if you marry a white person.

Where each parent lands inside that spectrum depends on several factors. One is nearness to immigration. As a general rule, the closer to the immigrant experience, the harder it is to have your children marry outside your nationality. A second factor is the nationality. Japanese Americans, for example, have the highest "outmarriage" rate of all Asian Americans.

A much higher percentage of Asian American women outmarry than Asian American men. Thus, there is a controversial third factor: why do Asian American women prefer non-Asian American men to Asian American men? This issue is discussed in chapter seven.

A fourth pressure point for Asian American children can be to stay within their social community. For Korean Americans especially, this is often the church. For others it may be ethnic associations or clubs, informal friendship networks, patronizing "our people's" businesses or marrying another person of the same ethnicity.

Feeling Pressure from Other Places

We cannot and must not blame our parents for all the pressure we feel. Yes, they are the source of some of it. Some of it, however, has other sources.

Some of the pressure felt by Asian American students and young adults are shared by all students and young adults. All of them face the pressure of succeeding in school. All deal with the uncertainty of marriage: if at all and to whom? All who claim Christ as Lord struggle with honoring him with all parts of their lives. As Asian Americans, we don't stand alone with these pressures.

In many Asian Americans, there is drivenness and a desire to do things perfectly. This creates a tremendous pressure to perform well. Sure, some of the pressure comes from our families, but there are other sources.

The Myth of the Model Minority

One source of the pressure is in being the "model minority," as Asian Americans are often described.

The label is hard to hide from as articles appear in newspapers and magazines with titles like "Why Asians Are Going to the Head of the Class," "The Triumph of Asian Americans" or "Outwhiting the Whites." The articles describe us as a people who have overcome racial adversity and poverty to attend the nation's best schools and climb the corporate ladder without complaint or protest. (Between the lines the articles say, "Why can't African Americans and certain Hispanic Americans overcome their stuff like the Asian Americans?")

Let us collectively debunk this myth that we are the model minority. Not only is it a slam on other ethnic minorities, but it is simply not true.

In 1989 the median family income for Asian Americans was $41,583, while for Caucasians it was only slightly higher. Because more Asian Americans live in extended family households, this figure includes the incomes of all persons living under one roof, which means that not all Asian American individuals have jobs that pay as much as or more than Caucasians' jobs.

Additionally, in 1989 11.4 percent of Asian Americans lived below poverty level, compared with 9.9 percent of all other Americans. Asian Americans are not just the successful Japanese American businessman driving the Lexus. They are also the poor, elderly Chinese American man who occasionally can afford bus fare to leave his cramped Chinatown apartment.

In the education arena, Bob H. Suzuki, president of California State Polytechnic University at Pomona, writes in "Model Minority,"

> The vast majority of Asian students are not superbright, highly motivated overachievers who come from well-to-do families. Large numbers of them are encountering personal or academic difficulties; many, especially those who have recently immigrated, are struggling to learn English.

He continues,

> The few Asian counselors to be found in higher education report that many Asian students are undergoing extreme psychological

stress and alienation. For some students, the pressures become so great that their academic performance suffers, sometimes forcing them to drop out of school. These psychological problems have been exacerbated by incidents of racial harassment and even violence against Asian students on several campuses across the country. (*Change* 7 [November/December 1989])

Somehow, and sometimes unconsciously, Asian Americans have come to believe all the press about being the model minority. We see this impossibly high standard and compulsively feel that we have to achieve it.

Another part of the myth is that all Asian Americans excel in math and science. Not true. Not true. Not true.

While some certainly do excel in those subjects, there are many of us who do not. For us math means turning on a calculator, and science is knowing what kind of fish that is in my sushi. We would prefer writing a rap song or reading eighteenth-century French literature or experimenting on a soufflé.

In a recent talk I gave, I mentioned receiving a D in business math my freshman year. Later an Asian American student approached me with a huge grin. "I'm so happy you got a D in math. Now I can tell my dad that since our speaker got a D, I can too!"

A second source of pressure is internal, meaning that it comes from within. Perhaps we take our parents' expectations and blow them up some more. Or maybe we let the Model Minority stuff get to us.

Mary Li Hsu, assistant dean of Yale College and director of the Asian-American Cultural Center, says, "Living with the expectation of being perfect—especially in math and science—is an enormous burden that can cause emotional problems for some [Asian American] students." She adds that it is not uncommon to see an Asian American student "implode" under the pressure. "There's a lot of depression going on." According to a study done by Iwa Ministries, Asian Americans have the lowest self-esteem of any demographic group in the country.

Such pressure has its price. Lavannya Raman, an ethnic counselor for freshmen at Yale, sees a lack of self-confidence stemming from the pressures of having to succeed. "There are a lot of expectations placed on students by society and their families, and they fear that they can't live up to it. It's just a myth that all Asian Americans are well-adjusted" (quoted in Jennifer Kaylin, "Myths of the 'Model Minority,'" *Yale,* February 1995).

As a high-school sophomore, I had little to show for myself. I was providing little for my younger siblings to look up to. I was an average student and an average athlete. When things got rough, I usually quit and moved on to something else. But something grabbed me that fall. I had one of those "kairos moments" that only a high-school student can have. Perhaps it was a song on the radio or the burrito I ate. I made a decision: *I will never quit again! I will succeed! I will win!* I felt my family and all my aunts, uncles and cousins cheering me on.

I worked after school in the employees' cafeteria at the Western Electric plant in nearby Sunnyvale. I scrubbed pots and pans and mopped floors. On this one epiphanous day, I was working alone. I had a huge, heavy garbage can to lift. On previous encounters with this can, I would usually lift it a few inches, grunt and put it down, leaving the garbage to smell overnight. But on this day I struggled with that

> **Our prayers are often like this:**
>
> Jesus, how could you accept me? I'm so awful. I'm a failure. I can never please my parents. I will follow you when I become a better person.
>
> What Jesus tells us is "I love you and I accept you—just as you are. You don't have to make yourself better to come to me. Just come."
>
> Jesus, I am so ashamed that I have failed. I never get it right. I am such a worm.
>
> Yet Jesus' message to us is "You are going to blow it. You will fail. You don't have to do it perfectly. I can live with that. I forgive you. Get up."
>
> Jesus, I never please Dad. Mom always finds fault with my grades. I just can't live up to their expectations of me.
>
> Jesus tells us, "You're right. You can't always please your parents. Instead, find your identity first in me. Yes, your family is important, but pleasing me is more important."

can. I yelled at the top of my lungs, "Don't quit! Don't give up! Never give up again!" I was sure all my samurai heritage (if I had any) was coming forth at that moment.

I prevailed over that garbage can that day, but there would be many, many more cans to lift in my life. As I went on in life, I found that I could not lift them all. In fact, in my effort to be perfect and to complete everything I set out to do, I was dropping more and more cans and the garbage was stinking. Something had to change.

Lifting More Cans, or Receiving Grace

As Asian Americans, we do not need any more exhortations to "lift that can!" or "graduate at the top of your class!" or "never do anything to shame our family!" We have been exhorted. We know how tall the mountain is and how difficult it is to climb. We need something else.

At the heart of Jesus' message is acceptance, grace and forgiveness.

Jesus wants to take all the heavy "cans" we are trying to lift on our own and bring them to the foot of the cross. At the cross there are no illusions. None of us is able, or was created, to lift all those cans by ourselves. Jesus died so that we can put the cans down. His death "lifts" those cans for us.

A Long Obedience in the Same Direction

Eugene Peterson wrote a great book with a wonderful title, *A Long Obedience in the Same Direction.* In it he looks at following Jesus as a lifelong journey. Big changes don't come overnight, but they do come as we give ourselves to Jesus for all of our lives. Asian Americans need to see growth and development as "a long obedience." We won't get it right the first time and every time, but that is all right. What is important is that we give our lives to Jesus for him to overhaul over the long haul.

"I am confident of this, that the one who began a good work among you will bring it to completion by the day of Jesus Christ" (Philippians 1:6).

BRYAN COLLEGE LIBRARY

2

Your Parents Love You, My Parents Love Me

Jeanette Yep

IT WAS RAINING. EVERYBODY ELSE, IT SEEMED, HAD A MOM WHO came to pick them up in the family station wagon after school. Not the Yeps. My grandfather walked the half-mile to our elementary school in the rain to "pick up" my brother and me. He carried his big black umbrella and wore his *I'm proud of you two* grandfather smile as he met us at the edge of the schoolyard. We greeted him in Chinese, "Ah yeh, ni hao ma?" (Grandfather, how are you?).

But then Bruce's mom caught my eye. She offered my brother and me a ride home. I looked at Grandpa. I looked at her station wagon full of my schoolmates. "Yes, thanks!"

Speeding off, I looked through the back window and saw Grandfather slowly walking home, grandchildrenless under the shelter of his big black umbrella.

Grandpa died at age ninety-three. He had immigrated to the East Coast in 1901, at the end of the Qing dynasty in imperial China. He was one of the first Chinese to settle in Boston's Chinatown. He was a simple man. He never had much formal education and could barely read and write. But he had an uncanny way of affirming each of his grandchildren. Whether he was building us a kite out of sticks we had gathered and rice paper he had bought in Chinatown, or carving us a bow and arrow to "shoot" one another with, Grandpa was there for us. He knew how to spend time with us. He spoiled us and hung around with us. Grandpa was a great playmate!

Work Hard—Be Obedient

My parents, on the other hand, were busy trying to discipline and raise us, busy trying to earn a living, busy trying to decipher American life and culture. It was easy to misunderstand and misinterpret their intentions. It was easy to think they were concerned only about my grades, how well I compared with my cousins and extended family, and whether or not I was an obedient daughter. Some days, when I would reflect on the adolescent antics of some of my friends, I thought my folks should be a lot more grateful to have a "good kid" like me—respectful, honest, earnest, hardworking, studious. Instead of gratitude, I got the "all A's, but oh, here's a B—can't you do better?" speech, or the "you're not such hot stuff" speech, which usually went something like this: "Mrs. Moy's daughter Karen is not only on the math team, but she won Miss Chinatown U.S.A. Karen plays her flute for the youth symphony and vacuums the whole house weekly before Mrs. Moy has to ask."

I remember once trying to persuade my parents that good grades should be rewarded monetarily, just as my friends' parents rewarded their grades. My father said, "Are you crazy? Don't you know that getting good grades is *your* work? You want us to give you money for it? What about all *our* sacrifices for you children?" I had to think of other ways to earn money. Grades would not be the route of choice in our family.

Since elementary school, I've taken off in many other station wagons. And I have often left my parents behind on the sidewalk of the Donald E. Ross Elementary School. From there they watched me travel away from the family nest. Ironically, many of the station wagons that have captured my affection are the result of my parents' sacrifices and gifts—my college education, my friendships, my opportunities for world travel and my vocational choice of Christian ministry. Some of my elective "road trips" have unintentionally hurt them (such as how I announced I was going to Taiwan after college graduation, instead of letting them into my thinking about this before it was a fait accompli).

My parents have watched me leave home (somewhat ungracefully) and have watched me make choices as a young adult—some good ones and some bad ones. They have been there to bail me out, to lend me money to buy my first car, to help me with rent and food. And they have not moved from the sidewalk of the Ross School, wanting to express their love and yet not always knowing how to respond to me and my decisions.

Over time I realized that I should explain more about why I was taking all these trips in various station wagons with all kinds of other people, but mostly without *them*. And I continue to learn more ways of expressing my love back to them. This chapter is a bit of a travel guide, pointing out some of the landmarks and land mines on the journey.

Discovering the Love

Understanding and believing that my parents love me has been a lifelong process. I have never doubted that they want good for me. I have always had enough to eat and wear; a warm, safe house and lots of academic encouragement. I enjoyed enrichment opportunities such as music lessons and organized sports teams—things my parents couldn't even dream about when they were growing up in wartime China and Depression-era America. I have always known about and (most of the time) been grateful for the extensive sacrifices they made for the sake of the family. They gave up the familiar and known ways of China and Myanmar (formerly Burma) to move to a new land, the "Golden Mountain" (as old-time Chinese refer to America). They took on the risks of relocating, of being culturally and personally displaced, of not knowing the language. They endured racial prejudice and discrimination. Why? Primarily so that my siblings and I could have better opportunities in life.

In traditional China, family roles were clearly defined. Parents were parents. They disciplined and admonished the children. And children were children. They were to honor, behave, obey and never cause the family to "lose face." Affirmation for the young would most readily come from other adults in the extended family—grandparents, aunts, uncles and close family friends. Mom and Dad didn't have the job of affirming the children. They reasoned that if they did too much of that, the children might end up spoiled.

I saw my father perform the job of affirming my cousins. He was their favorite uncle. They were the same age as us kids, but my cousins sought my dad out for counsel, advice and help. My dad freely affirmed them. He told them they were doing great in school. He encouraged them to be more helpful at home. My siblings and I were totally puzzled. "How come Dad doesn't talk to us like he does to our cousins?" Looking back, I realize that we didn't understand the marked difference between his role as our father and his role as an uncle.

My parents raised us to the best of their abilities. As parents, they wanted to ensure that my generation would not suffer as they had. They sometimes tried to motivate us to succeed through stories of deprivation. I think their reasoning went something like this: "If the kids know how much we suffered, they will be more grateful and will be more likely to work harder. Working harder means better grades. Better grades mean better colleges. Better colleges mean better job opportunities and marriages."

While I was younger, I didn't particularly like the stories of hardship and deprivation. Once when I was told to finish my meal because my aunties and cousins in the People's Republic of China would eagerly eat even the scraps from our table, I responded cheekily in Chinese: "Great! If they want this stuff, why don't we just box it up and send it to them in China?" That comment earned me a quick one-way ticket to my room! (Only one of my many pilgrimages to that special room.)

Our family had an annual ritual to recall hardship and to "eat bitterness" (as it is said in Chinese). Each December the whole family (including our huge German shepherd, Yep-Yep) piled into the car to see the Christmas lights on Boston Common. As we got closer to downtown Boston, the car always took a detour to climb the "back" side of Beacon Hill (an affluent neighborhood where many of Boston's socially prominent types live). We kids knew what was next. From the back seat rose the thoughts: *Oh no! Here come the years-of-sacrifice-and-deprivation stories. Help, pull the ripcord!*

Sure enough, driving up Beacon Hill immediately activated a memory chip in my dad's mind. "Children," he'd start. We knew we were in for a speech.

"Children, your father never said no to education. He was always grateful for the chances he had to be in school. Grandpa and I worked in that building—see that basement apartment—look, Ma, it's now a hot-dog stand! I'd clean the clothes the sailors would bring us. I would iron the shirts and uniforms, wait on customers, do whatever needed doing. Then, in the morning, I'd go up Beacon Hill to deliver the bundles of laundry to all the rich people before I went to school. You kids should stop your complaining and be grateful that your only work is going to school."

After a few more fatherly comments that would make Horatio Alger proud, we finally turned the corner and headed for the Christmas lights.

Between Imperial China and Boston

Although I did not enjoy these tales of "eating bitterness," they became, over time, trust-building, loving and learning opportunities between parent and child. My folks needed me to know and care about *their* stories. I needed to learn how my mom hid in the hills of southern China with my oldest sister when the Japanese warplanes flew overhead. And how Dad and Grandpa sacrificed so that my second uncle could attend the local community college, Harvard University. I needed to know about their childhoods, their joys and disappointments. These accounts gave me perspective and helped me understand and appreciate them better. And these same hardship stories offered clues to my parents' love for me.

Struggling to survive, having a foot between the old world of imperial China and the new world of Boston, likely led to much uncertainty for my parents about how to raise up a family in America. "Should the kids be fully Americanized?" or "Should the kids be fully Chinese?" "What does 'Chinese American' look like?" I'm sure my folks would have appreciated my turning out more culturally Chinese than American, but hot dogs have a way of poisoning your mind and cultural values!

I never doubted that my folks loved me enough to meet my material and physical needs. But, I confess, I've sometimes doubted their love, because often they didn't seem to know how to meet my emotional and psychological needs. There were many moments in my growing-up and adult years that my folks just didn't seem to "be there for me" in ways I would have liked. For me, one of the implications of growing up biculturally in America has been the need for more emotional, expressive encouragement and support than my immigrant parents knew how to give. This hunger for expressions of love from parent figures was intense at times.

One weekend in college, I visited the home of a European American classmate. Mary Kay's family was a touchy-feely, huggy type. Various family members would often have their arms around each other, and her mother even sat on her dad's lap in the family room! They verbalized how much they loved and appreciated one another. Mother expressed how much she missed Mary Kay. Dad expressed how proud he was of her achievements at college. Mary Kay's little sister said how quiet their home was now that she had left for school. Their dinner discussion exuded warmth, mutual respect and love.

What a contrast to family mealtimes at our house! What a contrast to the way I related to my parents! My folks would always be my parents. We would not be "friends." Dinnertime conversations usually revolved around the meal itself—"Ah, this fish is steamed just right"— what our relatives did and didn't do correctly, and perhaps a few questions directed toward the children about how school was going. Our family seldom shows physical affection. In fact, when my dad hugged me the first time as he said goodby to me my freshman year, I remember thinking, *I'm choking for air. Why is he doing this?*

The more I got to know my college friends, the more I realized that my parents were different. There were a lot of contrasts between our Asian home and their European American ones. I became angry at God for not dealing me a better hand. Didn't God know that I had emotional needs too? Didn't he know that I was hungering for parental approval and acceptance expressed in a way that spoke to my heart? Didn't God know that I was tired of being compared to other Chinese overachievers?

Over time God has healed this ache. I know that my parents love me. They aren't perfect parents—and I'm certainly not a perfect daughter! They weren't parented perfectly, and they didn't parent me perfectly.

Steps to Healing

How did I get to the place where I could accept and could begin to reconcile the tensions I experienced in relating to my parents? A couple of things helped.

First, I grew in my understanding and appreciation of my parents' background and culture.

Without being fully aware of my motives, I became an East Asian studies major, studying Chinese history and art history. I started on the long, painful (incomplete) trek to learn how to read, write and speak Mandarin. Reading Chinese classical literature, exploring Confucius's *Analects* and delving into Chinese civilization began to provide the cultural context for my parents' "weirdness." I studied China's five thousand years of continuous history, especially devouring the period surrounding my family's immigration to America, the time of China's war with Japan and Chairman Mao's communist revolution. That helped me understand better why Grandfather immigrated when he did, why my father is a card-carrying Republican and why my folks buy American and dislike the communist Chinese regime.

After graduation from college, I spent a year in Taiwan. While there, I had opportunities to visit several other Asian countries. One summer day, I was in the home of a Hong Kong relative. Something was spilled onto the floor. Instinctively, my cousin reached for a rag that was in the corner of the kitchen. Using her foot to direct the rag, she wiped up the spill with a few quick swipes of her right foot.

Egads! I thought. *That's exactly what my mother would do back in Boston!* Back home in the States, I had never seen anyone else use a rag and a foot to mop up a spill. Then it dawned on me. What I thought was a pretty weird, non-Donna Reed-like housekeeping activity was normative for my Chinese family members still living in Asia. It wasn't that my Chinese parents were inherently "weird" or "different." No. They just seemed it in contrast to dominant-culture America.

Something else that has helped me realize my parents really do love me is understanding that they speak a different language of love.

I intentionally began to look for ways they expressed love to me. Let me explain. Judson Swihart in *How Do You Say "I Love You?"* suggests that people "speak," or use, varying "languages" to express their love. These languages of love include meeting material needs, helping each other, spending time together, meeting emotional needs, saying it with words, saying it with touch, being on the same side and bringing out the best in the other person. Each of us "speaks" some of these languages of love with fluency. Others of these languages we speak more haltingly. Swihart's point is that we need to recognize this difference—to try, as much as possible, to recognize which languages we speak most readily and then to gain fluency in another's language of love.

In a time when I was diagnosed with clinical depression, one of my big issues was understanding and accepting how my parents expressed love to me. While working on these issues in therapy, I had a dream. My mother was offering me a meal. I asked her in Chinese, "Do you love me?"

"Silly girl!" she said in Chinese, sounding slightly annoyed while busily shoveling more food into my rice bowl. "I feed you, don't I?"

This dialogue, in my mind's eye, helped me realize beyond a shadow of a doubt how my mother showed her love for me. It was a message I desperately needed to hear. This dream breakthrough was one of the ways God allowed me to receive her love for me. My parents speak fluently the love-language of providing for my physical and material needs.

In addition to this therapeutic breakthrough, I've intentionally chosen to forgive them for hurts (known and unknown to them) done to me. (Joan Guest's pamphlet *Forgiving Your Parents* has been helpful on this topic.) I have identified some of the points of pain, invited Jesus into and imagined him in these situations with me, and prayed for God's healing of the hurt. I've sought professional counseling, accepted the loving gift of empathic listening from friends, and received healing prayer.

I'd be lying if I said I have totally forgiven and forgotten. I'd also be lying if I said the aches are as deep and the sorrows as profound as they were in the past. God is good. He has healed and continues to heal me. I love my parents, and I know that they love me, warts and all.

The Family of God

These cognitive understandings still don't replace my hunger for verbal affirmation, for honest conversations about feelings and for my parents just to tell me that I'm the world's best kid, hands down! God met my real, emotional parental need through the church. Through the family of God, I have, in some ways, been "reparented." With the help and encouragement of caring adults and friends I call my surrogate parents, I've had some deep emotional needs met, and I've learned that my parents do love me.

In my junior year in college, God brought into my life a couple with big hearts. Each Sunday, they went out of their way to pick up students in our InterVarsity chapter to drive us to church. Being local IV supporters, they frequently invited us back to their home for Sunday lunch. During exam times they opened their living room for us to study in. The whole time I was observing Don and Lynn. I saw how they related to one another and to their kids. I saw how they were generous with their possessions and time. I saw that they knew how to be serious about their faith and yet they also knew how to have fun. In particular I was attracted to Lynn's honesty and ability to ask hard questions. Don was the steady wisdom and balance in their family and marriage. Over time we became friends.

Don and Lynn were from my parents' generation, but they loved me in ways my parents couldn't. From them I received verbal affirmation, honest feedback and challenges to grow and mature in Christ. Many times, through tearful conversations, Don and Lynn would provide perspective on my parents' actions, which I just couldn't understand and often found so hurtful. One time when Lynn and I were sitting in a rowboat together she asked, "Jeanette, do you think you are responsible for your parents' happiness?" Other times they would explain some of the pains and fears parents have as they raise their children and watch them make choices as young adults. Through their questions, through their perspective and maturity in Christ, through countless conversations and meals, and in other ways I can't really pinpoint, my friendship with Don and Lynn helped me grow to more fully accept and believe that my parents do love me.

God is good. His extended family, the church, was the human means for me to grow.

Tips for the Return Trip

Believe me, I've not yet "arrived" in relating to my parents! I've been working on this for a long time. (The converse is even more true, I'm sure!) At one of the lowest points, I remember thinking that I'd never go back home again. I would be polite to my parents, but I just would avoid them—after all, I was an adult and I lived twelve hundred miles away! My wise therapist put a quick end to my all-or-nothing thinking. Instead, she helped me come up with a strategy for how to better manage my trips home. Whether you live near your parents or far away, these tips may help you relate to your folks and help you better survive potentially difficult trips home.

☐ *Write a letter to your parents periodically.* Despite my extroverted tendencies, we just never talked much about matters of substance at home. There was a huge linguistic chasm. My mom speaks only Chinese, and I know "kitchen Chinglish," which is woefully inadequate to express more meaningful emotions and concepts, let alone any nuanced thoughts or feelings. My dad is bilingual, though. He would read my letters and then translate them for my mom. (I know enough Chinese to defend myself, to know if he was too free in his editorializing or if he was sticking to the text. This kept the communication honest!)

Through letters, I've been able to communicate adult and some-times other, more difficult things. In turn, they have gotten a chance to learn more about my thinking and decision-making process. In letters I've been freer to express my love and appreciation for them. At times I've even sent some downright mushy cards and notes. Letter writing has helped our relationship. I wish I had made more time for it!

☐ *Clearly define your trip's purpose, its duration and your expectations in advance.* Like all InterVarsity staff, I raise my financial support. Some of my supporting churches and partners in ministry are back home, close to where my parents live. It used to drive my folks and me wacky when I'd come home. "What meals will you take here?" "Shall I come get you at the airport?" "Do you need the car?" "Here are some of your phone messages already." And the young adult's favorite, "What time will you be home?" Now I work hard at setting appropriate expectations before I arrive. I've found mixed trips (business and pleasure) pretty undoable. So now I come home to do my InterVarsity things, *or* I come home to visit the family. Stating in advance my expectations for a trip has been helpful.

I've learned to rent a car in order to avoid some of the potential transportation conflicts when merging my parents' schedule with my own. I try to speak their languages of love and spend time with them. (I limit my phone calls and visits to friends. Otherwise, I end up just making my parents' home a pit stop, which, understandably, vexes them to no end.) I try to help them in some practical ways as well. On some trips I've painted, wallpapered, mowed the lawn, helped out with tax preparation, cooked, cleaned or shopped. This tangible help gets me big points!

For me more frequent, shorter trips are better. It costs me more in airfare, but it saves me therapist money! Before I head home, I ask some close friends to pray for my visit, that I'll be patient and gracious, that I'll be able to be God's person in my parents' lives. This may sound a bit overblown. After all, these are my parents—they love me, and I love them. But as a result, I have found that trips home are becoming easier, and I dread them less as I apply some of these principles.

You Can Change!

You can't change your parents. You *can* change your own attitudes toward them.

There have been times when I've been tempted to despair that my relationship with my folks would ever get better. I've wondered where God is in my pain. In those times I've honestly not been able to be hopeful for my relationship with my parents. In those times God has graciously given me the gift of some "hope bearers," often friends with the gift of faith who have prayed for and believed God's best for me and my parents. They've expressed the hope of Christ for me in my life situation when I could not muster the faith to do so for myself. I thank God for the gift of these hope bearers. God can do all things (even when I lack the faith to believe this). He can change you and your attitude toward your parents. He continues to do so for me.

The journey to understanding my parents' love for me has been quite a ride! There are still smooth places and bumpy sections where I need an off-road-equipped vehicle. There have been friends who've journeyed with me—some within the church family (like Don and Lynn), some within my extended family (like Grandpa)—and some extraordinary resources from God's Holy Spirit (like being able to forgive and receive healing for painful memories).

As my parents and I age, we have mellowed, have learned from mistakes and are growing in grace. I give thanks to God for them. In my heart of hearts, I know that they love me. Do you know that your parents, however imperfectly, love you too?

3

Honor & Obey

....

Greg Jao

CHRIS BEGAN OUR CONVERSATION WITH AN APOLOGY AND A NER-vous smile. "I always cry when I think about my kitchen-table encounters with my parents," she warned, "so don't be alarmed."

A bright, articulate and successful finance major at a private Midwestern university, Chris described her parents' reaction to her decision to teach in the inner city after graduation instead of working in business. "Mom seemed so disappointed, and Dad just got angry. He kept telling me that I could support inner-city schools better if I were a successful businesswoman, that this is just a phase, and that I shouldn't be such a fanatic about my faith."

She looked up suddenly and added, "I mean, my parents are Christians. They just don't understand. I worked for an inner-city mission this summer. I know that God wants me to be a teacher. And I know that it would kill my parents if I didn't go into business. After all, what would my aunties say?"

I sympathized with Chris's problem. My parents and I had argued about similar issues for the past six years. At my parents' request I had attended law school and was practicing law when I met Chris. However, I had believed all along that God wanted me to pursue student ministry with InterVarsity. We were at an impasse, just like Chris and her parents.

As we continued to talk, Chris revealed that past conflicts with her parents over schools, boyfriends and extracurricular activities had been played out at the kitchen table as well. "My non-Asian friends tell me I need to do what is right for me. And they tell me that I need to love Jesus more than I love my family. But the youth pastor at my home church says the Bible tells me to honor and obey my parents.

"My parents tell me what to do, and I always concede. My non-Asian friends think I'm crazy for letting them run my life. And I'm beginning to wonder if they're right."

She paused and rubbed a few tears from her eyes. "No one understands. Everyone is telling me to do something different. What should I do?"

Between Two Worlds

Chris faced a painfully common problem. To help her better understand the issues, we began to discuss the difference between Asian and Western decision-making priorities and orientations.

Influenced by Confucius's teachings on filial piety and hierarchy, traditional Asian cultures value duty and obligation as the highest motive for making decisions. Mature Asians recognize and accept their social responsibilities. In contrast, modern Western cultures believe an individual's self-actualization is the highest motive for decision-making. Mature Westerners act consistently with their self-understanding. Therefore doing something "because I should" or "because it is expected" and not "because it feels right or honest to me" suggests maturity in traditional Asian cultures and immaturity in modern Western cultures. Because of these differing cultural priorities, Chris felt torn between her responsibility to her parents and her responsibility to herself.

Chris also felt pulled by different cultural orientations. Traditional Asian cultures have a group orientation. The group—whether family, clan or country—defines the individual's identity and destiny. In contrast, Western cultures generally demonstrate an individualistic orientation. The independent self defines its identity and destiny. (This summary is adapted from Connor, *Tradition and Change in Three Generations of Japanese Americans.*)

The distinctive orientations of Asian and Western shape each culture. For example, group-oriented Chinese names often are composed of three characters. The first character, the "family name," identifies our family or clan, and the second character often marks which generation of the family we belong to. The third—and last—character distinguishes us from our siblings and cousins, identifying us as individuals. The order of the characters reveals the lower priority given to individual identity and the higher priority placed on group identity. In contrast, Western cultures reverse the word order. They usually use the "first name" to distinguish an individual from the group and any remaining names to identify the individual as a member of a family or clan. The different cultural orientations affect the way Asians and non-Asians participate in our decision-making.

Chris thought about this information for a while. "So what you're telling me is that because of my parents' group orientation, they assume they have not only the right but also the responsibility to shape my plans?"

"Yes," I replied. "For them, love requires that they play an active and influential role in your decision-making. From their perspective, only abusive or unloving parents would remain detached and encourage autonomous decision-making."

"And for my friends?"

"For your culturally Western friends, love requires that they encourage autonomy and self-fulfillment. True love would encourage your individual choice."

"I think I get it," she said slowly. "My parents and friends operate with different cultural orientations, so they're giving me conflicting advice. But both groups are being consistent with their own cultural priorities and orientations." I nodded.

"But what about the different Scripture passages. Are you saying those are culturally determined too?"

Between Two Commands
Chris's friends and youth pastor quoted different passages of Scripture to her. Her non-Asian friends cited Jesus' statement that he came "to

set a man against his father, and a daughter against her mother, and a daughter-in-law against her mother-in-law; and one's foes will be members of one's own household. Whoever loves father or mother more than me is not worthy of me" (Matthew 10:35-37). On the other hand, her Asian youth pastor quoted Paul's command "Children, obey your parents in the Lord, for this is right. 'Honor your father and mother'—this is the first commandment with a promise" (Ephesians 6:1-2).

Her counselors' choice of verses reflects their cultural biases. Displaying an individualistic understanding of faith, her non-Asian friends quoted verses that emphasize an individual's response to Christ. They found it hard to understand why it was difficult for her to give priority to God's call. On the other hand, her Asian youth pastor, with his group orientation, cited verses emphasizing group responsibility. If God had called her to work in the inner city, he reasoned, he would give her parents peace with her decision. His Confucian cultural roots shaped his orientation. For example, Confucius stated, "In serving his father and mother, a man may gently remonstrate with them. But if he sees that he has failed to change their opinion, he should resume an attitude of deference and not thwart them; he may feel discouraged, but not resentful" (*Analects* 4.18).

As a Christian, Chris wanted to submit herself to the teaching of Scripture. As an Asian American, she wanted to take both passages of Scripture equally seriously. As an individual faced with a decision, she was stuck. We began to study the two passages.

An Absolute, Surprising Obedience

The apostle Paul issues two commands to obey and to honor parents: Colossians 3:20 and Ephesians 6:1-2. The apostle uses broad, absolute language, commanding children to "obey your parents in everything" (Colossians 3:20), and bases his teaching on the fifth commandment (Ephesians 6:2), natural law (Ephesians 6:1) and Christian obedience (Colossians 3:20). For Paul, divine revelation, general revelation and Christian experience collectively confirm that children must obey the commands of their parents. His commands provide no clear exception to the reach of a parent's authority. Pastor R. C. Lucas notes, "We are wise to acknowledge the force of Paul's all-embracing language, and not to jump too eagerly to the task of dismantling it by finding exceptions" *(The Message of Colossians and Philemon).*

Because Paul's commands are general ethical teachings, we shouldn't be surprised that he doesn't provide exceptions. "Is it not characteristic of Paul to give a basic rule for the churches without qualification, leaving it to experience and spiritual wisdom to discover the inevitable limitations of such rules?" adds Lucas.

For example, Paul was not requiring obedience in abusive situations. Unfortunately, some Asian parents are physically, emotionally, sexually or spiritually abusive. Misguided church leaders often require children to obey parents in any situation. And with their group orientation, Asian churches encourage this kind of unquestioning obedience. Scripture does not. Experience and wisdom indicate that abused children should seek protection, not offer submission.

It is important to recognize the context of Paul's teaching. He writes to a Christian audience in both epistles. The apostle assumes, therefore, that the commands issued by parents and obeyed by children will be commands consistent with scriptural principles and oriented to kingdom priorities.

Notice that Paul's teaching on parents and children occurs within a larger section that regulates relationships within the New Testament home: husband-wife, slave-master and child-parent (Ephesians 5:21—6:9; Colossians 3:18—4:1). Within these sections, Paul imposes complementary restrictions and obligations on each party. The complementary nature of the obligations significantly recasts the seemingly absolute nature of the commands. To New Testament (and Asian) audiences, Paul's command to children would be uncontroversial. Fathers in New Testament times had absolute authority over children (A. Skevington Wood, "Ephesians," in *The Expositor's Bible Commentary,* vol. 11). According to Dionysius of Halicarnassus, a writer at the time of the early church, fathers could imprison, enslave, scourge or kill their children under Roman law, regardless of the child's age (cited in Markus Barth and Helmut Blanke, *Colossians).*

In contrast, New Testament fathers (and many Asian fathers) would find Paul's directive to avoiding exasperating (Ephesians 6:4), embittering or discouraging (Colossians 3:21) their children revolutionary, incomprehensible and unnatural. Almost no moral, legal or ethical teaching of the time limited a father's power over his children. Yet far from providing a parent with absolute authority over a child's decisions, Scripture significantly limits a parent's power. According to Paul, a parent's commands not only must comport with Scripture but also must be sensitive to the emotional impact of the commands on the child. The assumption: a parent's commands will be wise, scriptural and gentle.

After we had studied Paul's commands, Chris looked pained. "Aren't there any other exceptions? I mean, what if I am already an adult? What if my parents aren't Christians? What if they're just wrong?"

I smiled ruefully. "You're mostly out of luck."

Elderly Children and Disobedient Parents

Some have read Paul's positive command to parents ("bring [children] up in the discipline and instruction of the Lord," Ephesians 6:4) to mean that the parents' authority applies only while they are responsible for the spiritual, moral and ethical education of their children. Once the parents' responsibility ceases, the child's responsibility to obey the parents ceases as well.

Jewish believers like those at Ephesus might have assumed that a child's obligation to obey his or her parents would have ended at or near age thirteen. At that age Jewish sons were regarded as independently responsible members of the religious and legal community and were eligible to marry (J. A. Thompson, *Handbook of Life in Bible Times,* citing Rabbi Eleazar ben Simeon, who wrote in the second century A.D.). Within our cultural context and making these assumptions, children would be free of the obligation to obey their parents sometime in their mid to late twenties, when most children reach their legal majority and marry.

It also would be logical for a parent's near-absolute authority over a child to cease at the time the child gains an ability to marry. In Christ's teaching on marriage in Matthew 19:4-6, he affirms the priority of a person's marital relationship over his or her relationship with parents, noting that at marriage children leave their parents and become bound to another. And in the culture of Jesus' day, almost all individuals would have been married by their late teen years. (For a facinating discussion of marriage patterns in Scripture, see Clapp, *Families at the Crossroads,* chap. 5.)

However, New Testament scholar Markus Barth points out that Paul cites the fifth commandment ("honor your father and mother") in support of his teaching in Ephesians. The fifth commandment applied to grown children, who would have lived under their father's authority until his death. Barth also notes that contemporary Greek texts used the term translated "children" to refer to children of every age—adult and infant. Other contemporary Greek texts applied Paul's terms for "training" or "raising up children" to children who were adults; therefore his teaching could not apply merely to "young people" (Barth and Blanke, *Colossians*). As Dionysius of Halicarnassus points out, the authority of parents to discipline their children was unquestioned, even when it was applied by parents against adult magistrates, government officials and noted citizens (ibid.). It seems unlikely, therefore, that either marriage or adulthood frees a child from the absolute duty of obedience.

Paul does not directly address situations in which parents are non-Christians. In contrast to his teaching on divorce (1 Corinthians 7:12-16), his teaching here does not change if one party in the parent-child relationship is a non-Christian. And it is unlikely that he would provide such an exception. Paul grounds his commands not only in divine revelation but also in natural law ("for this is right," Ephesians 6:1). Unlike his general teaching on holiness (for example, Colossians 3:1-11), the expectation that children should obey their parents is not necessarily based on the unique Christian identity of family members. Philo, a secular Jewish philosopher contemporary with Paul, states that children could obey parents in everything because "the true father will give no instruction to his son that is foreign to virtue" (Barth and

Blanke, *Colossians,* citing Philo *De Specialibus Legibus* 2.236).

Similarly, Paul's understanding of secular authority suggests that he would not create exceptions for non-Christian parents. In Romans 13 he states that God has established secular governments for the purpose of restraining evil and therefore those governments should be obeyed (Romans 13:1-3). By analogy Paul would argue that non-Christian parents have similar God-given responsibility for children, and in general, their properly given commands should be obeyed.

Paul also refrains from making our obedience conditional on a parent's prior obedience to Christ. He does not say, "Children, obey your parents *if* they refrain from exasperating you." He addresses children directly in the second person, treating them as independent moral agents.

I could not control my parents' unfavorable response to my desire to do ministry, and their response was not my responsibility. My responsibility was to choose how I would respond to them. When I felt that they were being unreasonable or unfair, I had to choose to respond with grace, obedience and humility. And when I failed to respond properly, as I often did, the responsibility for failure lay with me alone. A Christian's obedience is never conditioned on another individual's prior obedience.

After we talked through these issues, Chris sat in silence for a while. Her next question helped me appreciate the depth of her commitment to Christ. "But if I must obey, how do I obey hard commands without becoming bitter? Do I just have to grit my teeth and bear it?"

I smiled. "No, I don't think so. By citing the fifth commandment in Ephesians, Paul's teaching challenges not only our behavior ('obey') but also our attitude ('honor'). It reminds me of the Sermon on the Mount: God demands external and internal conformity—integrity—in our actions. Bitter obedience or slavish disobedience isn't an option." We turned back to Scripture.

The Discipline of Obedience
Paul's teaching on family relationships begins with the command "Be subject to one another *out of reverence for Christ"* (Ephesians 5:21).

The prepositional phrase makes all the difference. Our obedience arises from and in the context of Christian discipleship. We obey out of our love for and commitment to Christ. In the end, we are submitting to Christ and not merely conceding to our parents' desires. Paul reemphasizes this truth in Colosians by calling children to obey their parents "in the Lord" (Colossians 3:20). Theologian John Stott notes the prepositional phrases "bring child-obedience into the realm of specifically Christian duty, and lay upon children the responsibility to obey their parents because of their personal relationship to the Lord Jesus Christ" *(The Message of Ephesians)*.

In effect, it is Christ, not our parents, that we obey. Our obedience can be joyful, sincere and dutiful, then, because it is chosen out of love for Christ and not imposed by our parents or required by our culture.

Because it was important for my parents that I have a graduate degree and professional work experience, I went to law school and practiced law for two years before pursuing ministry, as a way of honoring them. Their biggest fear was that I would resent them. Initially I *was* mad. But because I was motivated by a desire to obey Christ, I could not—and did not—remain mad while I took finals or crammed for the bar exam. Because I chose to obey Christ, I was free from the temptation to be bitter or frustrated. Instead I remained involved with students, tried to grow in character and maturity, developed skills that aid me in my current ministry, and picked up an extra degree, new friends and great work experience.

After this discussion, it was clear a hard question was bubbling in Chris's mind. Almost apologetically, she asked, "This may seem presumptuous, but what about Jesus' statements? You waited six years to obey what you believed to be his call. How did you justify that?"

"That's a fair question. But I think my response is consistent with Jesus' overall teaching. I don't think Jesus and Paul are being inconsistent."

An Obedient Hatred
In his teaching and lifestyle, Jesus emphasizes the priority of the kingdom of God and the exclusive nature of his authority over the life

of the believer. To the disciple who asked to bury his father in obedience to the fifth commandment, Jesus responds, "Let the dead bury their own dead" (Luke 9:59-60; Clapp, *Families at the Crossroads*). To the disciple who asked to say goodby to his family first, Jesus replies that those with competing obligations are not fit for his company (Luke 9:61-62). In response to Jesus' exclusive call, the disciples James and John enact an Asian parent's nightmare: they abandon their family business, leave their father with the hired help and follow Jesus (Mark 1:19-20). Highlighting the contrast between the biological family and the family of Christ, Jesus states, "Whoever comes to me and does not hate father and mother, wife and children, brothers and sisters, yes, and even life itself, cannot be my disciple" (Luke 14:26). Jesus brought a sword, not peace, to the biological family (Matthew 10:21, 34).

Jesus himself, in his interaction with his own family, models the primacy that must be given to the kingdom of God. Luke emphasizes how the boy Jesus gave priority to God's work *before* he describes Christ's obedience to his parents (Luke 2:41-52). Jesus respectfully chides his mother about the nature of his mission *before* transforming the water into wine in Cana (John 2:1-12). And when Jesus' mother and brothers try to end his ministry and retrieve him because they think he is crazy, Jesus rebukes them. He asks, "Who are my mother and my brothers?" His answer: "Whoever does the will of God is my brother and sister and mother" (Mark 3:33, 35). Theologian of the family Rodney Clapp notes, "If Mary and her other children cannot accept Jesus' vocation, he cannot recognize their kindredness. Mary comes as a mother; her son calls her to something even more fundamental— he calls her to discipleship" *(Families at the Crossroads)*.

In his actions and statements, Jesus places the biological family in a position of secondary importance to the kingdom of God. Clapp states, "It is the new first family, a family of [Christ's] followers, that now demands primary allegiance." Christ, his purposes, his Word and his people provide the framework within which we make our decisions.

Because our primary loyalty is to Christ and because our obedience to parents arises in the context of Christian discipleship ("in the Lord"), we may not and cannot obey commands that are incompatible with Christ's commands. Commenting on Paul's seemingly absolute command to obey, Stott asserts, "The submission required is to God's authority delegated to human beings. If, therefore, they misuse their God-given authority (*e.g.*, by commanding what God forbids or forbidding what God commands), then our duty is no longer conscientiously to submit, but conscientiously to refuse to do so" *(The Message of Ephesians)*.

But the conflict between God's commands and our parents' commands must be genuine and immediate before we refuse to obey our parents. By condemning the abuse of Corban, Jesus repudiates using religion to avoid obedience (Mark 7:9-13). By declaring property or funds Corban, individuals dedicated the item to God's use in the temple. Items declared Corban could not be used for other purposes. Thus unscrupulous children could withhold their land, property or funds from needy parents by declaring those items Corban.

Jesus' condemnation of the abuse of Corban demands that we exercise great care before assuming that our parents' orders conflict with God's commands. A genuine conflict does not exist unless our parents' demands contradict God's desire for an immediate, specific and absolute response. Stott would advise Christians whose parents oppose their baptism, for example, to wait for years before being baptized, because God's command to be baptized does not require an immediate response. "Even baptism, though Jesus commanded it, can wait until you are older. . . . If, on the other hand, your parents were to forbid you to worship and follow Christ in your heart, this you could not obey" (ibid., p. 242).

Nonimmediate discipleship issues might include opportunities to attend conferences, participate in short-term missions projects or live within a specific Christian community. (In other circumstances, these opportunities may represent a specific lordship issue and require disobedience.) On the other hand, immediate, specific and absolute discipleship issues might include a parent's order to worship at a family altar, to leave offerings for family ancestors or to marry a non-Christian.

It is impossible to create a hard-and-fast rule to determine when disobedience is required. However, because our perceptions often are clouded by our own resentments, desires and passions, we need to engage in extensive prayerful reflection, thoughtful conversation with believers of various cultural backgrounds and ages, an in-depth and honest assessment of the issues and our desires, and a careful study of Scripture before choosing to disobey our parents. Paul Tokunaga often says, "We need to go all ten rounds with the issues before we decide to disobey. It needs to be a decision made slowly, carefully and prayerfully."

An Honorable Disobedience

Even when we might be called to disobey our parents, we can continue to honor them. The term *honor,* as used in the fifth commandment and by Paul in Ephesians, connotes a child's respect for the parent's position as parent and an appreciation for the standing and task of a parent's place in the social order (S. Aalen, "Glory, Honour," *New International Dictionary of New Testament Theology,* vol. 3). Honor requires that children protect a parent's dignity, attribute weight to a parent's counsel, acknowledge a parent's higher social position and respond appropriately to a parent's love and wisdom. Biblically, giving honor does not depend on a parent's worthiness or possession of positive parental attributes.

Scripture provides several examples of honorable disobedience. Ruth disobeyed Naomi and followed her back to Israel to demonstrate her love (Ruth 1:8-18). Jonathan, while protecting David, continued to serve and to honor his father, Saul (1 Samuel 18—20). Jesus himself honored without obeying at both the beginning and the end of his adult life. As a youth he remained at the temple to assert God's primacy but then recognized his secondary obedience to his parents (Luke 2:41-52), and on the cross he provided for his mother's support and companionship before abandoning her in death (John 19:25-27).

Often the cost of honoring our parents is high. Many Asian Americans have chosen to delay their marriages to people unacceptable to their parents. Others, having been disowned, consistently care for and attempt to communicate with unresponsive parents for years—or even decades. For at least three pastors I know, the choice to pursue ministry meant facing up to a parent's threat of suicide, attempting to communicate love and avoiding bitterness.

For John, honoring his emotionally and physically abusive parents first involved moving out of the family home. "I can't control them," he said one night over coffee. "But I can control—at least a little—their opportunities to be bad parents. In a funny way it honors them by helping them to be better parents."

He also has learned to forgive. "I used to try to excuse my parents by saying, 'They just had a hard day at work.' But I've come to realize that I can't excuse them; they're responsible for the abuse. They sinned against my sisters and me. But the Christian response to sin is to forgive." Still, John hasn't forgotten. "I don't think I really honor them by pretending that they didn't abuse us. It honors them more to treat them as responsible adults rather than as children incapable of controlling their tempers. You can't really honor someone with a lie."

Other times honoring our parents involves practical decisions. Some friends, faced with demands to worship at a family altar or engage in occult practices, have gone with their parents to the ancestral shrines to honor their parents, but have chosen not to participate in the ceremonies. In my case, I could not obey my parents' desire that I choose a career outside of InterVarsity, but I tried to communicate my desire to honor them. I waited six years—turning down or leaving two jobs, attending law school and then practicing law for two years—before I started working for InterVarsity. Within the context of a lifetime of ministry opportunities and in consideration of my parents' desires, a six-year delay did not seem unduly long or impractical. It communicated honor graphically and powerfully to my parents.

I also learned to hear both their stated and unstated concerns over our eight-year-long conversation about working for InterVarsity. Initially I thought they were being materialistic. Our conversations frequently revolved around money issues. "The languages of love" (described in chapter two) helped me understand that they were motivated by love. When they said, "How can you support yourself on an InterVarsity salary?" I learned to hear their unstated message: "We love you so much that we don't want you to go without." Hearing their love made it easier to bear the more painful conversations.

Through the years, my parents moved from aggressive rejection of my desire to work with InterVarsity through passive resignation and grudging acceptance to, most recently, supportive ambivalence. Similarly, I moved from angry frustration through resigned resentment to ambivalent appreciation. Throughout the process my parents have tried—often successfully—to communicate their love for and concern over me. I have tried—often less successfully—to communicate my desire to honor and to obey them.

The Conclusion to Obedience

As Chris and I finished our conversation, she said ruefully, "I never thought Christian obedience could be so complicated and so hard. And I never realized understanding Scripture could be so difficult. Has it been worth it?"

What I told Chris was that only recently, after being with InterVarsity for several years, I had begun to see the fruit of my attempts to honor my parents. My parents admit that the process has stretched their faith. They've challenged their own assumptions, dreams and plans. And they've begun to use our painful experiences to counsel other parents at our church.

And I know my experiences have deepened my ability to be obedient to Christ in difficult circumstances. I've also grown and changed. I've learned to wait, to listen and to trust.

My decision to be obedient and to show my parents honor—and their commitment to love me—gave us the chance to listen hard, speak honestly and commit ourselves to loving each other. We've become better disciples and a better family as a result. And together we've learned that nothing—not one tear, not one experience, not one hurt—has been wasted in God's economy.

4 Doctor or Lawyer?

Susan Cho Van Riesen

BRAD WAS A STUDENT IN THE LAST YEAR OF HIS M.D./PH.D. PRO-gram at a very prestigious medical school in California. After years of incredibly difficult work, the stress became too much. He "snapped" and decided to take some time off to hike around Europe. After one year, to the shock and dismay of his parents, Brad decided to scrap the whole M.D./Ph.D. plan and become a potter.

Michael, a straight-A student in an Ivy-League law school, has a good job waiting for him after he graduates. Yet he is deeply depressed because he's not interested in law, nor does he feel that God has put it on his heart for law to be his life's calling. Michael chose law over medicine because his parents made it clear that those were the only options for him. He would really like to go into full-time ministry, but he is afraid even to mention it to his parents out of fear that it would threaten his mother's fragile health.

Doctor, Lawyer or, Maybe, Engineer

Asian parents, especially recent immigrants, can have an extremely narrow view of the acceptable occupational choices for their children. Many parents hope or expect that their children will choose from a small list of high-level, respected professions, such as medicine, law, business (usually corporate) or education (usually higher education). In addition to prestige, salary and career security are often highly valued.

Many second- or "1.5"-generation (born there but grew up here) Asian Americans struggle with feeling incredible pressure in the area of making future decisions. Some fold under the pressure of expectations, while others may rebel.

Recently a *Los Angeles Times* article discussed the immense desire on the part of many Korean American parents for their children to go to Harvard University so that their children can secure high-paying and prestigious jobs in the future. The stories in this article illustrate the amount of pressure and high expectations Asian Americans can experience.

Some parents will go to great lengths to try to get their children accepted. One mother moved from Illinois to Massachusetts and lived apart from her husband while her son attended prep school. Another lived on her son's schedule, staying up late while he studied during his last two years at a Hollywood high school to give him snacks and lend moral support.

A few indulgent parents promise lavish rewards—a BMW being top prize—for a Harvard recruit. A few parents even name their sons Harvard and Yale for what they hope will be a psychological edge. (K. Connie Kang, "Korean American Dreams of Crimson")

The situation can become very tense, even volatile, when we pursue or even just consider a job that does not match our parents' values of societal respect and financial security. Many students who have felt led to go into full-time Christian work or social work have experienced much persecution and disappointment from their parents. Others struggle with a cultural perception that being a full-time pastor is the only way to serve God.

It's not only parents who seem to funnel Asian Americans down the narrow occupational track. Media images and stereotypes paint a picture of Asian students who always and only do well in science or math. Peter Cha, who ended up becoming a pastor with a master's degree in theology and a Ph.D. in sociology, remembers being voted "most scientific" in high school. "But I'm not scientific at all!" he says.

Understanding Our Parents

It is crucial, first, to attempt to understand where our parents are coming from in their perspectives on our career choices. For example, among Asian parents, providing well and having one's physical needs met in an ample and dignified way is of utmost importance.

When my sister was applying to colleges several years ago, she looked for schools that had a good conservatory or music department because she wanted to be a professional cellist. Despite her giftedness in music, her love for the cello, and the fact that my parents themselves had encouraged my sister to learn how to play the cello for the previous ten years, they strongly disapproved of her leanings. She had been accepted at Yale, but she wanted to go to Oberlin because of a better musical training situation for her. My parents thought she was crazy! Their clear concern was that a professional musician, unless extremely lucky, cannot look forward to a very financially stable future. One of the primary reasons my parents had moved from Korea to the United States—and suffered the immigrant experience in a foreign country—was so their children could have a comfortable lifestyle. "We don't want you to go through what we had to" was a refrain that we heard often growing up.

My sister and I had a hard time understanding what they were talking about most of the time. Because of their choices and accomplishments (and the grace of God), we had never lived through a wartime or postwar situation. We didn't know the lack and chaos of an underdeveloped economy. Most of our friends' parents were going to high-school dances here in the States while our parents were trying to reunite with their families following the Korean War. Education and good jobs were much more of a challenge to attain. As we gained perspective on their life journey, my sister and I began to understand why financial security was so important to our parents. They were not being randomly anxious about money. They simply had been deeply affected by their earlier experience of scarcity and difficulty.

Second, we struggle to communicate well with our parents because they may not share some of the values that may be assumed by this current, more "Americanized" generation. As Jeanette points out in chapter two, we often speak completely different "languages" from what our parents speak. A friend of mine remembers telling her mother during college that she wanted to do something after college that "would help her to get in touch with who she really was." Her mother, however, who had not been influenced by such a psychologically oriented, individualistic culture, had no concept or value for self-expression or psychological self-understanding. "I know who you are," she would reply. "You are my daughter. Study hard and get a good job."

Most of our parents' generation and cultural background emphasizes interconnectedness and filial piety, not self-understanding and self-acceptance. When a culture based on Confucian philosophy encounters a culture that has been deeply influenced by humanistic psychology, much confusion can result.

Caucasian American parents on TV and in the movies tell their children things like "Do whatever you really want to do; I will always support you" or "Whatever makes you happy makes me happy." Meanwhile, Asian American parents' constant chorus often is along the lines of "Mr. Lee's son went to Harvard and is going to be a doctor" or "Cousin So-and-so is going to law school. How happy his parents are."

It is tempting for those of us in the younger generation to conclude that our parents don't love us or want our true happiness. Actually, our parents love us very much, but their conceptions of what ultimately will make us happy differ from our own ideas (see chapter two).

Third, it is wise to keep in mind that our parents may hope to see some of their own aspirations and desires come true through the lives of their children. In the Asian mentality this is not as evil and manipulative a thing to do as it is in the mainstream American, individualistic society, where one's personal choice is the most important thing. Remember that in most Confucian-based Asian cultures, the concept of ancestors living through their descendants is a very familiar one.

The father of one friend overcame incredible odds to graduate from the top higher educational institution of Korea. He became a very respected pharmacist and eventually ran his own pharmacy. Convinced that he could make an even better life for himself and his family in the United States, my friend's father moved to the Los Angeles area. Because of the language barrier, Mr. Kim found that further education in the States was impossible, so he pursued owning a small business rather than transferring his pharmaceutical knowledge here. The family ran a liquor store in a suburb of Los Angeles and did quite well financially over the years. Because his life ended up being given to the successful but not very respectable business of owning a liquor store, however, Mr. Kim and his wife put much pressure on their children to "do better than we did" and "get the respectable career that we weren't able to have because we needed to make money for you."

Now, understanding where our parents may be coming from does not necessarily render all their actions or communications right or godly. Just as our parents' values may not match up to ours, so they also may not match up to Jesus' values. Jesus doesn't hail prestige as central to the life of a believer. Our Lord denounces hoarding money as foolish (Luke 12:15-21). Yet we should not then cast away all of our parents' concerns as invalid, for planning well for the sake of provision is a good thing (Proverbs 6:6-11). Laziness leads to shame and poverty (Proverbs 10:5).

The key to wise discernment begins with knowing what kingdom values are first, and then listening well to our parents for wisdom and reflections of the kingdom in what they are saying. When I was first called to come on staff with InterVarsity, I flew up to my parents' house and laid my situation before them. I asked them specific questions about what they thought and listened to all of their concerns. Then I went away and thought and prayed about all that they had said. Although my parents were not able, at that time, to give me their blessing, we were able to communicate about the matter peaceably and respectfully. I can happily say that now, seven years later, I am enjoying the richest, warmest relationship with my parents that I've ever had. The process of listening carefully to my parents at that critical juncture of my life produced a large part of that growth.

God the Provider

Our journey into the future and our lives of work must begin with seeking the guidance and wisdom of our heavenly and perfect Father. Throughout the Scriptures God makes it clear that if we trust him, he will guide us into a good and happy future that glorifies him and makes use of us as he has created us to be.

The psalmist reminds us of how God is able to provide for each of us personally even in the midst of difficult situations:

The LORD is my shepherd, I shall not want. . . .

You prepare a table before me

in the presence of my enemies;

you anoint my head with oil;

my cup overflows. (Psalm 23:1, 5)

Your God is a God who wants to provide for you! This is what he is about. Giving generously to his children is how he wants to relate to us.

The way that the father in the story of the prodigal son treats his son reveals his amazingly generous character, regardless of whether the child has been "good enough" or not. "But the father said to his slaves, 'Quickly, bring out a robe—the best one—and put it on him; put a ring on his finger and sandals on his feet. And get the fatted calf and kill it, and let us eat and celebrate' " (Luke 15:22-23).

In order to be able to trust God, we need a deep grasp of the truth of God's good character. He is on our side. He wants to throw parties for us. We are not alone in seeking provision for our lives. This may be difficult to grasp, especially for those of us who have had to be pretty independent in our relationships with our parents. Some of our parents have been very good at providing for us. Yet we should all remember that throughout the ages God is the One who has been upholding and giving life to those who love him. He is the One who has suffered the most on our behalf and has been hardest at work for our good. It is crucial for us to know and remember this in order to be able to trust God and make faithful key decisions.

God Our Guide
Cynthia is a Korean American young woman in her mid-twenties who feels immense pressure to "hurry up and find a good career" for herself.

Whereas her non-Asian friends in "Generation X" are experiencing a more relaxed process of growing up and finding out who they are, Cynthia feels like she needs to get on that successful career path right away. Her parents often remind her that they came to America in order for her to have a good (read: successful) life. Cynthia's brother already has graduated from medical school and is in his residency. Cynthia has a nice job, but she lives with the panicky feeling that she needs to know right now what she will do with her life.

Many of us who share Cynthia's situation respond by making commitments that we are unsure of (such as going to medical school before being certain that God wants us to be a doctor), or we freeze and become unsure of anything. We need a guide other than the power of pressure. We need a gentle hand of guidance that helps us to consider our desires and open up our options.

The good news is that God does not expect you to get it all figured out by yourself. Rather, God promises to give guidance to those who ask. James 1:5 tells us that God gives direction generously and un-grudgingly. He is "into" being our personal occupational counselor. He knows what's out there and he knows us well.

Here are a few things to keep in mind in letting God be your occupational counselor.

1. You have to begin by telling God what you want. He will work with this.

2. Don't just talk *at* him. Listen. Too many of us communicate with God as if we are sending postcards rather than having a face-to-face (or at least a phone) conversation. How has God spoken to you before? Through the wisdom of a friend or pastor? Through prayer times? Through the Scriptures? Go to God through these venues and aggres-sively solicit his advice.

3. Seek confirmation of your sense of God's leading through godly people whom you trust. These people may include your parents, pastor, friends and siblings. Too many people make decisions on their own and get into trouble. Proverbs 11:14 teaches that "where there is no guidance, a nation falls, but in an abundance of counselors there is safety."

Vocation and Work in God's Kingdom

The word *vocation* comes from a Latin word meaning "calling." Vocation, therefore, has less to do with what we do from day to day to earn a living and more to do with our primary purpose for living: what God has created and called us to be.

For anyone who follows Jesus, our call is to follow Jesus and to be involved in kingdom purposes. Jesus' promise to those who decided to follow him at the beginning of his ministry was not that he would make them excellent fishermen or successful carpenters. Rather, he called them into becoming the first Christians by saying, "Follow me, and I will make you fish for people" (Matthew 4:19). For us as Christians, being a part of the unfurling of the kingdom of God through loving others and leading them into truth should be the ultimate concern and purpose in our lives.

Many people make the mistake of mixing up "call" with "job," saying things like "I've always known that I was called to be a dentist." We should remember that no matter what job we have—to place ourselves in a situation that makes us most useful to the kingdom of God or to pay our bills—our identity should lie in our goal to be ministers of the gospel.

When John Wanamaker was U.S. postmaster general, he was actively involved in running the Sunday school of his church. He was asked, "How do you get the time to run the post office and the Sunday school too?"

He answered, "Why, the Sunday school is my business! All other things are just things. Forty-five years ago I decided that God's promise was sure: 'Seek ye first the kingdom of God, and his righteousness; and all these things will be added unto you.' " John Wanamaker is someone who understands what his vocation truly is!

Since the days of the early church, history has led us to an unfortunate understanding of the word *minister* as a professional, seminary-educated leader. This leads the rest of us to think that ministry is an extra, a volunteer aspect of our lives. Kingdom resources are often wasted because those who do not do official "ministry" simply pour all of their skills and talents into self-growth, success or making money. More Christians should see themselves as ministers first in whatever job they do and seek to maximize their effectiveness as kingdom workers, regardless of position or title.

AnaLiza worked for a large motor corporation as a receptionist for the billing department. She believed that her "call" was to be a Christian first, though her job was to be a good receptionist. As she prayed that she could apply this calling at her work, AnaLiza found God opening numerous opportunities to plant seeds of faith during phone conversations, as well as serving her coworkers by giving people rides home and praying for people she met at work. Her days became more life-giving and meaningful as she put her identity first in being a minister of the gospel. When she had to quit her job to go on a mission, AnaLiza found that she had enjoyed her work so deeply that she left with tears.

If we believe that God is everywhere, there is no such thing as a secular job. We should never think of our work as being separate from our lives of faith. Any job, as long as it is not in opposition to the laws of God, can be a matrix for our real, central call—to be fishers of men and women. Work should be an act of worship, a vehicle for purpose, creativity and joy rather than simply a utilitarian act in order to secure food, housing or education.

Problems come when we don't do this but rather put our trust in work as a source of hope and identity. We look to our jobs or professions to provide peace and security for this life. Yet no job, no matter how meaningful, esteemed or respected, can ultimately give us those things. Being a professional cannot protect us from the overwhelming evils of the world. Being an executive cannot promise us true joy.

Greg, a Korean Christian friend of mine, left college with no particular vision or values for involving God in his vocational life. He was very bright and landed a high-prestige, high-paying job in downtown Los Angeles. Now, seven years later, he has a very impressive car and bank account, but his relationship with God and the spiritual meaning of his life is quite shallow. He is very busy and uses most of his money on entertainment. Greg has lots of things that should, according to society, make him happy, but he is not. Frankly, lots of Asian Christians, like Greg, are turning into mere yuppies.

From Greg's story and the story of the rich young man in Mark 10:17-22, we are reminded that only God should be at the center of our lives. To give our work that place in our lives is idolatry. Christians should fight with all their heart to preserve Jesus' place as the One who gets the glory for giving us a good life.

Practical Suggestions for Honoring God *and* Your Parents

☐ *Trust that God is the One who has the best plan for your life.* If you have a hard time believing this, that God is the most perfect parent and the One to whom our allegiance goes first, you may want to take some time to have some people pray for you to grow in this area of discipleship. I have received much from taking a two-day personal retreat when I was in a perplexing decision-making process. Some people find that times of fasting (from food or talking) help them to focus on connecting with God.

☐ *Listen to your parents.* Are you able to articulate what their true concerns for you are? Can you talk to them about your future in the presence of a trusted friend and then hear your friend's perspective about what they seem to be saying and where they are coming from? Our parents are sinful, fallen people, so they are not automatic mouthpieces of God. Yet God can and often does speak through them. It is likely that you will find much wisdom in what they are saying if you are willing to listen well.

Practically, this means asking your parents well-thought-out questions in an honoring way that they can respond to. (For example, "Well, what are you going to say now about my life?" doesn't work as well as this approach: "Dad and Mom, I know that you have a lot of thoughts about my future and decisions that I need to make. I'd like to hear your thoughts about why you think grad school is a good next step.") Also, you may want to try just listening and not saying anything in reply until you've had a chance to go away to think and pray about what they have said. Interpretation is better done with some space from the conversation and time to pray rather than in the heat of the moment.

☐ *Don't use the Bible as a weapon.* Whether you know the Bible better than your parents or vice versa, waging theological battles, especially when the issues are primarily cultural, are not fruitful. Concentrate instead on personal dialogue. God is neither "on your side" nor "on your parents' side." Rather, God is interested in helping people to love each other and make faithful decisions.

☐ *Take advantage of advocates in talking with your parents.* When I wanted to go on my second summer mission in college, my parents had a hard time understanding why I would not use the time to get an internship in something more "career-strategic." I was blessed to have an older Korean pastor friend of the family take us all out to dinner and talk to us about why he valued missions and what he thought I could learn. It was a fabulous opportunity to have my convictions expressed to my family without being contrary or dishonoring. My parents eventually let me go and even ended up supporting me.

Are there any older people in authority whom your parents respect and who could connect with them on your behalf, who might be able to lend legitimacy to your plans and options that they don't like or understand? Is there someone with whom you can communicate well who can explain your parents' perspective to you? This might be a great opportunity to get help in speaking your parents' language of love. Perhaps a pastor, community leader or person in the profession you are interested in can gain a hearing with your parents that you, as their child, never could. When an InterVarsity staff director visited the parents of a Chinese American student leader, bringing a box of ginseng as a gift, it was an immediate "in," and the parents have been very trusting and fond of the staff director and IVCF for years since.

☐ *Show how you are being responsible in what you are considering.* My mother was greatly relieved to find out that InterVarsity Christian Fellowship is a reputable organization that is financially responsible. She was glad to know that when I came on staff, I did have life and health insurance, a pension plan and other "adult job" things.

Usually it's not that our parents simply hate "alternative" job choices, it's that they don't understand them and don't see how they are going to provide well for our futures.

Have you begun to think through how the career or area of work you are considering will meet your basic and supplementary needs?

What are your parents' perspectives on the basics in terms of salary, benefits, retirement and personal growth options? You should know what they are, so that you can work with this information respectfully and thoughtfully.

Also, have you asked about and thought about your parents' needs in terms of their future? Do they have a retirement plan? Did they invest that retirement money into your college education? What are their hopes and expectations regarding your providing for them? You may need to consider these factors in order to make plans responsibly. Jesus didn't appreciate people neglecting providing for their parents, especially in the name of "religion" (Mark 7:9-13).

□ *Consider a different timeline so that you and your family can be better prepared for the future you are stepping into.* You don't always have to do immediately what you sense you are being led to do. One young man I knew, who sensed that God wanted him to do ministry overseas building homes for the poor, took an office job for a few years. This job enabled him to pay off his student loans, and he also had time to work through issues with his family. As a result, he was eventually in a more stable position to go and serve.

Hudson Taylor, founder of China Inland Mission, warned about trying to take on a call in our timing and not God's.

It is a great comfort to me to know that God has called me to my work, putting me where I am and as I am. I have not sought this position, and I dare not leave it. He knows why he placed me here—whether to do, or learn, or suffer. Meanwhile, beware of the haste of the impatient, impetuous flesh, and of its disappointments and weariness.

Can you take an intentional "time of preparation" for what may come next? Make sure that you are connected with some people who will help you stick to your goals and vision for this time. They can help you avoid getting distracted and stuck.

□ *Let yourself dream, and get in touch with your real desires and interests.* Stasha felt guilty and embarrassed about her desire to go to law school. She was afraid that it was a selfish, worldly desire and that she might not be able to get in. Yet as she opened up to her pastor about her secret interest and prayed with him about it, they both began to gain a sense that this might be the leading of God, for several reasons. She is now saving money and taking the LSAT with the conviction that serving the urban environment (also an area of personal connection for her) through legal training just may be what God has in store for her.

Your desires may not necessarily or immediately be God's plan, but you should at least let them be in the mix so that you are being honest with yourself and everyone else involved. You are not doing

> ## Truths to Remember
>
> In order to keep from being tangled up in the ways of the world and wasting all that God has given us to use faithfully, two theological truths are crucial for us to remember.
> 1. God is the ultimate loving and providing parent. If you are in a trusting relationship with God, you never have to try to make it on your own. We can't earn our own way through life or earn our own way into his good graces. What God wants from us is dependence on him, especially regarding what we will do with our lives.
> 2. Your call is to be a minister of the gospel first and foremost, regardless of the specific job or profession you go into. To be of use to God in the spreading of his kingdom (through any job, not just "professional ministry") must be a primary consideration and motivation for any serious Christian.

anyone a favor by denying your own hopes and desires. Let them out. Write them down. Ask your friends if they would reflect and share with you what they think your strengths and weaknesses are. Talk and pray through your options to discern whether or not they are something God is giving you. If they are, it's God's responsibility to make a way for you. If you act in trust of him and are patient, he will lead you into his plan for you.

Danger: Decision Ahead

As Christians, we believe this world is not our home. We are merely sojourners on a long journey of redemption, seeking God's goodness and being a part of his work to bring others into the kingdom. Yet it is not right or possible merely to sit and wait to get to heaven. Hard work and useful labor are clearly parts of God's plan for us in this world. Jesus himself came into the world as one who worked and had a useful profession.

The process of discerning and entering into the work or profession that will be most useful in this sojourn on earth is difficult. Dealing faithfully with the hopes and expectations of our parents can be a most challenging venture. And we can easily be tempted to gain identity and security from our work rather than from God.

Have you ever thought about the incredible impact on the kingdom of God here on earth if more Asian Americans of this generation were free to be radically faithful in their vocational lives? It saddens me greatly to know that so many skills and gifts are tied up due to false expectations, difficult communication and materialism. Think of the immense educational and financial resources that could be freed up for the church, the poor and the work of the gospel! Our orientation toward hard work and perseverance could be a wonderful addition to ministry everywhere, from Third World missions to the corporate marketplace. There might be fewer doctors and lawyers around, but many more Asian Americans would be more peaceful and joyful in using their unique gifts to labor for the kingdom in this short time that we have here on earth.

May the God of all hope and power come and help us to let him lead us into faithful stewardship of our working lives.

5

Relating to Others— Understanding Yourself

Greg Jao

....

"I WAS PRETTY SURE I WAS GOING TO HAVE TO KILL HER," DEB JOKED over coffee. We were talking about Deb's relationship with Gina, her non-Asian roommate. Deb and Gina had roomed together for nearly a year before conflict broke out. Even though they shared interests, tastes and temperaments, subtle cultural signals nearly ruined their friendship.

"I was just being a good Asian. You know, when I'd see that Gina left dishes in the sink, I would just wash them and not say anything. It bothered me, but I figured it was no big deal. Nothing worth bringing up. But if I left hair in the tub even once, she'd yell at me. Then I'd get really mad because I'd be thinking, *I never yell at you when you don't do the dishes, so why are you yelling at me when I leave hair in the tub?* But I didn't say anything." Deb paused and took another sip of her coffee, grinning at the memories.

"I would feel pretty self-righteous and angry. I thought I was being the better Christian because I was sacrificing more for the friendship. So every time I did her dishes and every time she yelled at me about the hair, I'd stay quiet and get a little more self-righteous. It shocked Gina when I finally blew up, because she didn't know I was even mad. It took our big argument to help her realize that I found direct confrontation very hard to take, and that I wasn't going to tell her I was angry unless she asked. That's how I, as an Asian American, deal with conflict. It helped me understand that she wouldn't be offended if I needed to bring something up, and that I shouldn't be offended when she brought things up. That's how she does it differently. But the learning curve was steep!"

Friendships and interpersonal relationships involve much more than our cultural values. We build relationships on common experiences, similarities in personality or interests, opportunities for intimate sharing or geographic proximity. Our cultural values, however, can subtly affect the way we make and keep friends.

Making Choices, Making Friends

Asian and Western cultures prioritize contradictory values, as Paul Tokunaga discusses in the introductory chapter of this book. Western cultures tend to be more individualistic than the group-oriented Asian cultures. These contradictory values shape our understanding of our relationships.

A study conducted by Katherine Tuan-MacLean ("The Interracial Friendships of White and Asian College Students") has shown, for example, that Asian Americans most frequently define close friends as people who share the same values and feel like family. In contrast, whites define close friends as people with whom they share activities and intimate thoughts. The Asian definition focuses on the appreciation of often-unstated commonalities between friends. Many Asian Americans remark that they feel like they "just fit in" when they meet other Asian Americans. The non-Asian definition highlights individual interaction and expression between friends. The Asian definition looks at group formation, and the Western definition looks at individualistic expression. Not surprisingly, this study observed that Asians generally have fewer close friends than non-Asians.

These different values also shape the way we relate. Western cultures, for example, value individual achievement and self-actualization, best demonstrated in the Army advertising tag line "Be all that you can be." They also value self-expression and use confrontation: "If you don't like it, say something."

One non-Asian student told me, "I always feel too loud and too direct when I'm with my Asian American friends. I'm learning that I need to create room for them to speak—to be quiet—if I want to hear from them. And I need to be more tentative or indirect with my criticisms and comments."

In contrast, traditional Asian cultures value group identity and obligation. Their advertising tag line might read "Be all that your family has sacrificed for you to be." They also tend to be more deferential and avoid conflict. "Everything's fine," they may say with a smile.

Asian Americans, experiencing conflicting impulses from both cultural contexts, may find it difficult to decide how to act.

"I feel like a hypocrite," Jeff announced as we walked along the beach. "I act differently with my Asian friends than with my non-Asian friends. It's always bothered me because it seems dishonest. I mean, shouldn't I act the same way with everybody?"

Jeff had approached me in response to one of my talks on Asian American culture. I had briefly discussed the material Paul Tokunaga covers in the introductory chapter of this book, and he wanted to process the information. "What do you mean that you act 'differently'?" I asked.

He thought about it for a moment. "Well, this example's a little silly, but remember how you said Asians value deference and hierarchy? Then you said we often express that value at church by entering a room and immediately looking around to identify the grandmas and grandpas first?" I nodded. "I do that! I always look around and greet the appropriate grandparent first. But I wouldn't do that in a non-Asian setting." He turned and faced me. "So am I a hypocrite?"

I smiled. "No, I'd say that you're just acting maturely." He looked puzzled, so we continued to talk.

As I explained to Jeff, relational maturity involves making intentional decisions to respond to people in socially acceptable ways. Mature people, for example, choose not to indulge in a temper tantrum in public. Mature Asian Americans, I suggested, need to make decisions about how to act acceptably when we interact with Asian or non-Asian groups. We need to make choices to communicate in ways that people can understand. For example, my grandmother best understands my love when I treat her with deference and a respect for her place atop the family hierarchy. Treating her with informality and like a peer, as I currently do with my non-Asian former high-school teachers, would be hurtful to her.

As we begin to understand these conflicting impulses, I told Jeff, we're better equipped to recognize the reasons we relate to our friends and coworkers in certain ways. As we recognize these cultural impulses, we're better able to make appropriate choices about our responses. We learn to hear what they are trying to communicate, and we communicate what we want them to hear. Because we live in a predominantly Western context, four Asian cultural values seem to create the greatest relational dissonance: our group orientation, concern with face, conflict-avoiding tendencies and attention to hierarchy.

Thinking for a Billion and More

Hundreds of people had gathered for an international technology company's Asian American employee conference. While waiting to present a workshop later that afternoon, I decided to sit in on an employee relations discussion. "How would you describe your Asian American employees?" asked the facilitator. The dominant responses didn't surprise me: quiet, industrious, technical, family-oriented, respectful and harmonious.

The terms, the facilitator pointed out, reflect the strong group orientation of Asian cultures. Duty and obligation, rather than rights and privileges, provide the matrix for decision-making. Individual achievement is less valued than group achievement. As a result, non-Asian managers perceive Asian Americans as good team members. Conversely, they often don't perceive us as good leaders.

"Look at your list of terms," the facilitator directed. "These aren't terms that you associate with managers. In fact, Asian Americans hold less than 0.3 percent of senior management positions in the U.S., although we make up 3 percent of the U.S. population. The reality is that hard work begets more hard work—not promotions. Why? Because we don't come across as a manager-type people."

A friend who is a midlevel manager at that corporation confirmed the facilitator's remarks. "About 20 percent of our work force is Asian American," she noted. "But very few of us are senior-level managers. It has a lot to do with our working style." She explained that over a period of many years, her projects had consistently come in under budget, on time and above specification, but she never was promoted, although other members of her team were. Finally she went to her supervisor and asked why.

"I don't think it was a discrimination issue," she said. "But I pointed out that my management style is very Asian—I work to make my entire group look good. Our company, however, only rewards 'hotshots,' people who stand out and make themselves noticed. Finally I asked my supervisor who it made better sense for the company to recognize—someone who promotes himself or herself or someone who leverages the resources of the entire group."

"What happened?"

"I was promoted later that year." Recognizing the cultural differences helped my friend penetrate the bamboo ceiling that many Asians experienced at that company. She was able to identify—and help others identify—the differences in style that created a faulty perception of her managerial skills.

The group orientation of Asians also encourages humility and deference. As a result, the facilitator's list of terms didn't reflect a perception that Asian workers are aggressive or creative. "We're not a group of people good at self-promotion," a friend remarked. "It hasn't been modeled for us. When a friend would compliment Mom on my grades, my mom's immediate response was 'But her room is so messy and she never practices piano.'

"Now that example affects me at work. When the chair asks who has expertise to contribute to this project, it feels presumptuous to say, 'I'm good at that!' I want them to notice my competency on their own. But that's not how American business works. They just assume that I'm slow to volunteer or lack the basic skills."

Finally, some sociologists suggest that non-Westerners are slower to make commitments and decisions because of a group orientation. We recognize that our decisions affect others in our relational networks. As a result, we take more time to think through the implications of our actions. The needs of others may take significant priority over our own desires. We work hard for other people.

Protecting the Perceptions

Our group orientation also causes us to value saving face—preserving the dignity, identity and appearance of ourselves or our families. This is much more than a superficial concern with image, however. Losing face in a group-oriented culture changes our identity. As we lose the appearance of dignity, we lose the substance of dignity as well. As a result, Asian cultures typically avoid putting people in a position in which they might lose face.

In many Asian cultures, for example, it is impolite and improper to ask for help directly. Asking for help causes us to lose face because we must acknowledge personal inadequacy. It also places the other person in a precarious position. To acquiesce to the request is to accept a potentially burdensome obligation. To refuse, however, would seem selfish, causing a loss of face. Instead, many Asian cultures ask for help indirectly.

One Sunday, for example, the youth pastor might look troubled while talking with a group of adults. "What's wrong?" someone asks.

The youth pastor replies, "Oh, I'm a little worried. We need someone to help drive some youth group members to our retreat this weekend, but I don't know of anyone who has the time."

In this way the word subtly gets out. Everyone in the room knows that the youth pastor is asking for someone to volunteer. In typical Asian style, however, no one is directly and individually on the spot. It would be equally appropriate to volunteer or to express sympathy for the problem without volunteering. No one is put in the position of having to say that they won't take the time.

Positively, this concern for face encourages Asians to act empathically and proactively. We value meeting the needs of others before they ask. We express mutuality in our friendships by anticipating needs or desires—bringing gifts, picking up the tab at a restaurant or volunteering help before we've been asked. And we assume that others will provide help without being asked directly.

In a Western context, by contrast, we express mutuality by serving and asking to be served. In more highly individualistic Western cultures, offering help prior to a request can feel paternalistic. And help must be requested and refused directly. Many non-Asians wouldn't have heard the youth pastor's statement as a request for help. In fact, Asian indirect methods often sound like statements of fact rather than requests for help. It's not surprising that some non-Asians find Asians to be vague and unclear about their needs.

"When I was the vice president of the dorm, some of the non-Asian guys used to call me the dorm geisha," one Asian American friend recalls. "There were no sexual connotations. They were merely observing the fact that I did all of the little tasks to make the dorm social life better by myself. It didn't occur to me to ask for help. I just thought everyone would just step in to do something. But they didn't."

Negatively, concern for face can leave Asian Americans overly concerned with maintaining the proper appearance. As I drafted this chapter, I had another heartbreaking conversation with a Chinese woman on the West Coast. We speak regularly. Her daughter, who attends a local university, has walked away from faith. "She always says that Christians are hypocrites. Her experience has been that our church discriminates against people who are less intelligent or less talented. And it's true," the woman noted. "We valued education more than faith. I've heard parents say, 'If our daughter's grades drop, we're pulling her out of the youth group.' Our church didn't really have a place for kids who are different."

Preserving face also may encourage superficiality in our relationships. Although we delight in the ease with which we can form relationships with other Asian Americans, our concern for face militates against significant self-revelation of faults, weaknesses or hurts. We don't want to lose face by sharing these unacceptable problems.

This lack of self-disclosure can particularly damage our crosscultural friendships. Anthony Giddens, an Oxford sociologist, points out that postmodern cultures like those in the West value "pure relationships" in which trust is built through self-disclosure. The result: our non-Asian friends do not feel that they know us. "A lot of my friends ask about me and my family," noted a student as we talked in a local diner. "But I usually just say that everything is okay. It's too complicated to explain all of the weirdness of an Asian family to them." As we continued to talk, I wasn't surprised to find that she had few non-Asian friends.

Conflict Avoidance

Face, and perhaps the immense population density in Asia, causes Asian cultures to be highly motivated to avoid conflict. Asians handle conflict indirectly, often through unofficial intermediaries. In many families, for example, an older relative or family friend mediates between people in conflict. Meeting individually and casually with each party, the intermediary often subtly and indirectly advocates the other party's position. Soon the intermediary has the story from both parties and has relayed the feelings and thoughts of each person to the other. Within the Asian context and among people who understand the system, these indirect methods of confrontation permit both parties to express their grievances while avoiding a public confrontation, and yet the conflict gets resolved.

In crosscultural relationships, however, Asian conflict avoidance can *create* conflict, as Deb and Gina discovered. In multiethnic settings, Asian Americans and non-Asian Americans often struggle with their different styles of responding to conflict. To non-Asian Americans, we can seem unwilling to deal with the real problem, whether organizational, spiritual or emotional. They can accuse us of being unwilling to confront people under the biblical guidelines of Matthew 18. To Asian Americans, others can seem needlessly confrontational or insufficiently accommodating. We can accuse them of being unwilling to exercise patience or forbearance.

A non-Asian student noted, "My Asian friends seem so uncomfortable when we encounter conflict directly. They often want to back away or just accommodate me. I've learned to be more indirect—to speak in the past tense or more dispassionately—when I need to talk about conflict. It makes them more comfortable. And I've challenged them to be more direct when they're angry with me, because conflict doesn't offend me."

As part of our conflict-avoiding complex, Asian cultures also stress accommodation rather than competition. In some Asian communities, people don't express a preference for one option over another when they suspect another member of the party has strong preferences. To do so would force the party with the stronger preference either to veto the suggestion (causing them to seem insensitive) or to acquiesce in a choice they don't like. In crosscultural settings where this assumption isn't shared, accommodation can create relational stress, as I experienced with my friend Michael.

We were making plans to vacation together when he asked, with a little bit of exasperation, "Don't you have any opinions about where we go or what we do?" I indicated that I didn't.

"Is that 'No, I really don't have a preference,' or 'No, I really do have a preference but I'm just not telling you because I'm being Asian and it's impolite to tell you'?" he asked.

I shrugged, but he wasn't satisfied. "You know, it's a little frustrating traveling with you, because I feel like I have to make all the decisions. And I'm afraid that we're not going to do anything you want to do because you're being too polite."

Can I Say "You Stink"?

Our conflict-avoiding tendencies, coupled with a respect for hierarchy, can especially complicate crosscultural managerial relationships. I remember speaking to a non-Asian manager who said, "I found it very frustrating to work with Asian employees because I would never know what they were thinking. I was always wondering if they were lying."

I winced. "It's not the 'inscrutable Asian face' thing, is it?"

"No," he said with a frown, "but I don't know how to manage them. When I asked them how things were going, they would smile and say that everything was OK. Much later I'd find out that they were very unhappy with the supervision I was providing. I didn't know what to do. I asked them several times if there were things I could do to be more effective, and they always said no."

His feelings didn't surprise me. I've been involved in conversations with Asian American employees who had similar types of supervisors. "My supervisor is really nice," they usually say. "And he always asks if there is anything he should be doing differently to supervise me better. But what am I supposed to say? 'Your supervisory skills stink'? I can't do that to my manager—he's nearly as old as my dad."

Because Western cultures value at least the façade of egalitarianism in their relationships, many managers fail to recognize that the Asian value of hierarchy militates against an employee's being able to communicate disapproval. Similar dynamics often cause teachers to remark how "quiet" their Asian American students are and managers to remark how Asian Americans often don't participate in group discussions.

"It's hard to break out of our conditioning," one student noted at a retreat. "When I was little, I was told not to talk back. You're not really encouraged to comment or critique your parents or people who are older." But recognizing our tendencies gives us freedom to choose how to respond.

"My roommate always accuses me of being passive," another woman said. "She's always telling me to fight for my rights and tell others what I think. But I've always known I wasn't passive. Knowing a little about Asian conflict-avoidance tendencies really helps me understand why I act the way I do. It also helps me think more realistically about how I can make decisions to act differently."

Evolving Identities

Some of us feel trapped by the way we relate. On the one hand, we may act "Asian" with our Westernized friends, and we watch as our relationships founder or run aground on the miscommunication that results. On the other hand, we may act "Western" among our families and immigrant churches and experience the storm of disapproval and controversy that arises. Even though we rationally know we should choose to act more helpfully, we cannot. To act differently, we rationalize, would be to sell out.

Asian Americans need to identify and embrace both our Asian and our Western cultural background. When we fail to integrate the Asian and Western aspects of our personalities, we deny ourselves some of the multicultural tools that we have and that we need to live in a multicultural society. We end up responding to people only in a single way, playing only a single note of the cultural symphony to which we have been exposed. As a result, we feel uncomfortable in one cultural context or the other. When we accept and recognize aspects of both cultures as part of our heritage, however, we can move freely from culture to culture. But both internal and external pressures can prevent this integration.

Internally, we often have an evolving appreciation of our bicultural identity. It's easier to choose to be one or the other: be Asian or be Western. But our churches and our parents want us to be Asian. And everyone else wants us to be and to act Western. The resulting pressure can make us uncomfortable. Frequently our response to this pressure tracks our developmental stage.

Young children often do not recognize ethnic or gender distinctions with any degree of clarity or meaning. As they begin to differentiate and identify with certain groups—by gender or age, for example—they also begin to notice differences and identify with ethnic groups. Frequently there is discomfort as they recognize their difference.

As Janet and I ate lunch together one afternoon, she recalled an incident from sixth grade. "I remember that the teacher said, 'Now all of you will check the top box, except Janet, who will mark the box that says "Asian" next to it. You see,' the teacher said, 'all of you are Caucasians, with the exception of you, Janet.' "

Janet took another bite of her sandwich and swallowed before she continued. "I'd always had a subconscious understanding that my family was from a distant land across the ocean where everybody ate rice for dinner, even though I was born in Washington State. As I walked away from the classroom, I realized that I was different from every single person in that room. I was no longer one of the group. I was the exception to the rule. And I hated myself because of it."

Entering junior high and high school, most people experience the intense desire to fit into a group, even if the group is a group of nonconformists. At this time many Asian Americans respond to our ethnic differences with a denial or hatred of our Asian cultural heritage. Often the effects of ethnic self-hatred last into the college years. Most commonly this disdain is expressed first against the physical characteristics that distinguish us from the majority culture.

"I've always been uncomfortable being Korean," sobbed Rachel quietly as she shared with the group. We were at a student retreat. "When I was younger, I hated that my parents talked funny, that we ate different food and that our house smelled different. I hated looking different, and I wanted blond hair and blue eyes just so I would fit in. I was a 'twinkie' or 'banana.' You know, yellow on the outside but white on the inside." From around the room came a few laughs of nervous self-recognition.

"It's so hard! Now that I'm older, I feel like people don't take me as seriously because I'm petite. My friends who are pediatricians tell me no one will believe that they are doctors. Everyone thinks they're candy stripers."

Rachel's self-ambivalence was aggravated by feeling trapped in different cultural expectations. "Koreans have a phrase, *yahm jun hae.* It's a description of the proper demure female," she explained. "You know, you don't look up when you speak, you cover your mouth when you giggle, and you bow your head and smile when you say no." Both Korean and non-Korean women in the group nodded in recognition of the archetypal demure Asian female. "But that just isn't me. And it's not what American culture values. But if I don't act that way at church, people think my parents have failed in raising me."

Jason expressed a complementary response as an Asian male. "When I first came to college I was angry," he shared. "I was angry at the media, which portrayed Asian men as either effeminate wimps or kung-fu warriors. I was angry at Asian women and non-Asian guys for dating and making us feel castrated. And I was angry at non-Asian women for refusing to date us. And I was angry at myself for letting them all bother me."

Our ambivalence with our physical appearance, in combination with the academic pressure we experience, can create intense psychological stress. A colleague at a private university has noticed that her Asian American students suffer a significantly higher rate of anorexia and bulimia than her non-Asian students. Officials at that same university confirm that 80 percent of their emergency psychiatric calls come from Asian American students, even though Asian Americans constitute less than 20 percent of the campus community.

At other times we express our ethnic denial and self-hatred spiritually. At each of the last three Urbana conventions, for example, the second student to share in front of all eighteen thousand delegates has identified ethnic self-hatred as his or her biggest challenge. One Asian American student said, "As I saw Asian Americans up on stage, I began to realize that it was very uncomfortable for me to see them up there. . . . God showed me that it was because I did not trust them, and I did not believe that God loved Asians."

During the college years, as we work to define our identity more clearly, some people in ethnic denial often respond to the cultural dissonance by rejecting the dominant culture. We may seek a stronger identification with our Asian roots or with a vague pan-Asian identity and reject our Western heritage. Frequently, however, a trip to Asia disillusions us. "You know, I read books where the protagonist goes back to some Asian country and realizes, *These are my people!* That wasn't my experience at all," one student confessed with a laugh. "I thought I would go back and find people just like me. Instead, I found that I didn't belong there either. Nor did they want me. I was too Western for Asia and too Asian for the West. I just didn't fit in."

Fitting In

Our ethnic denial may not be entirely internally driven. Externally, the dominant culture encourages us to assimilate and make no waves, as recent English-only legislation demonstrates. In fact, politicians often laud Asians as a "model minority" group that has attempted to mainstream quickly. On a more "micro level," even our friends can unintentionally encourage us to submerge our ethnic identity.

Michael and I had roomed together for over a year and had been friends for nearly three when he expressed his bemusement over my interest in Asian American issues. "When I see you, I don't see an Asian American," he said. "I just see Greg."

I knew he meant it both as a compliment and as an assertion of his lack of racism. Michael genuinely didn't think of me as an Asian American.

"But I *am* Asian American," I replied. "It's a part of who I am. You may not see it because I work very hard to respond to things at the apartment in a pretty Western way. But there's a part of me that I don't express when I'm with you." As I said it, I realized the extent to which I had submerged my ethnic identity to accommodate the expectations of my roommates. Somewhere I had crossed from adjusting my expectations to communicate to denying who I was in order to fit in. But I learned that I wasn't the only one who felt the loss.

"I don't know that you're being fair—either to yourself or to me," Michael commented after he had thought about it. "It sounds like you don't trust me to learn to adjust to your Asian side. But I don't think I or anyone else will unless you give us the chance. And I want you to be free to be who you are—Asian and American. That's part of friendship too." He was right.

It was appropriate for me to choose to communicate and relate in a more Westernized manner while I lived with Michael. In the earlier days of living together, I don't think he would have understood my Asian communication patterns. But I did both Michael and myself a disservice by failing to gradually express who I was as an Asian as our relationship developed. I shared only those parts of me that I thought were appropriate, and as a result, our friendship didn't extend further.

Our Responses, Our Choices

We need to grow in our ability to accept and to integrate our Asian and Western cultural heritages. As we begin to acknowledge and integrate both, we gain control of responses. Our ethnic denial or pride begins to break down. We begin to celebrate who God made us to be.

The student at Urbana who explained how his ethnic denial affected his spirituality concluded by saying, "I talked to one of the speakers tonight, and he said, 'I think that there are two sides of you. There's an American side and an Asian side. God has really grown you in your American side, but a lot of your Asian side has been buried down under the ground.' I think that God is showing me . . . that God loves Asians and Asians do love God."

As we grow in our understanding of the Asian influences that shape our relationships, we gain the ability to identify them in action and make choices about whether or not to express these tendencies. They no longer master us. Instead, we can capitalize on them to cross cultures more smoothly or to shape our responses to better communicate our thoughts and concerns. We can be conflict avoiding or confrontational, direct or indirect, expressive or deferential, hierarchical or egalitarian, as the situation demands. We grow in wholeness and in our ability to express all of who we are in our friendships and relationships. And our Creator rejoices.

6
Marriage & Singleness

Peter Cha &
Susan Cho Van Riesen

IT WAS 3:00 A.M., BUT OUR DISCUSSION WAS LIVELY AND INTENSE. Thursday-night discipleship meetings, where I (Peter) met with a dozen upper-class men from our Asian American InterVarsity chapter to discuss a chapter from Temptations Men Face, usually ended around 1:00 a.m. But that night we were talking about dating, sex and marriage, and our meeting did not end until 4:00.

We shared honestly about issues such as why men in our fellowship didn't ask women out on dates. We laughed together about how sex is one topic that is completely and creatively avoided in our homes and churches. We asked each other some hard questions ("Have you thought about an interracial marriage?"). And we admitted our fears ("What would happen if the person I marry is the right person for my parents but the wrong person for me? Can I spend the rest of my life with someone I don't love?"). You can see why we were up all night.

As we were leaving the dorm room, one Korean American guy said, "I can't talk to my parents about these things, and I don't feel comfortable bringing up these topics with my Korean pastor. I'm glad we had this talk." It's been five years since that night, and some of my former students have continued to discuss those important issues with me, remembering that first talk with fondness.

Endless Matchmaking

My (Susan's) phone rang at 7:00 a.m.—again. The Korean pastor's voice was cheerful and full of confidence that I'd appreciate his news. "A very nice young pastor's son in Chicago," he said. "I have sent him your picture, and I think that he would be a good match for you."

The moment I graduated from college and told my parents that I wasn't going to graduate school right away, the project began. Get Susan married as soon as possible! Unfortunately, God did not seem to have the same objective in mind. I was also aware that there were ways I wanted to grow as a person and heal as a woman before I entered again into any serious relationship, much less marriage. Yet the cultural values swirled around me—and so did the comments and plans of a thousand "helpful" aunties and uncles.

In most families from Confucian-based cultures, the final responsibility of a parent is to marry their child to a good spouse with good credentials and family. Unlike Western culture, Asian culture sees the process of marriage as a very communal endeavor. The idea that a young person would "just find someone who I happen to fall in love with who is right for me" seems unreasonable and dangerous to many Asian parents. Therefore, often an entire extended community can become involved in the matchmaking process, through either active involvement or merely expressing strong interest in the situation.

The social clock (the communal understanding of when people are supposed to make life decisions) of Asian cultures is often earlier and stricter than that of the more individualistic Western cultures. This is especially true for women. I remember having a strong sense that the older people at my church were thinking, *Tsk, twenty-five already and not married yet!* though many of my Caucasian women friends of this age were focused on career, ministry training and further education before marriage. Truly the timeline of this generation does not match that of more traditionalist cultures.

Additionally, Asian men often struggle with a sense of a dynastic duty to father the next generation. One single Chinese friend lamented to me that every time his parents bought a baby shower gift for one of their many church friends who were having children, his father would smile and say aloud, "One day we will buy these for our grandchildren!" (No pressure.)

Trusting God

How can a person who is not married or not dating hold on to peace and the reality of God in the midst of this situation? Some of us want to be married and are trusting God for a spouse in his timing. Others of us sense a call to be single for a time or for the long term. For all single people, the key lies in trusting that God gives the resources to live faithfully in any given situation.

We Are Family

The strong "family feel" of many Asian churches can lead to a tremendous amount of pressure for Asian American young adults. Some end up feeling very unloved because of other people's overly zealous desire to press them into marriage. One friend of mine confessed, "Sometimes I feel like they don't care if I marry a duck as long as it has the right credentials!"

I (Susan) remember going to hear a speaker on the topic of marriage and singleness during my senior year of college. He asked, "How many of you here are married?" (One person raised his hand.) "How many of you think that you have the gift of singleness?" We all shrank back in uncomfortable silence. *(Oh please, not me, Lord.)* No one raised a hand. "You are all wrong!" the speaker said. "As long as you don't have the gift of marriage, you have the gift of singleness and all of its blessings and benefits."

Christians today need to be reminded that singleness is a valid biblical option with tremendous, respectable blessings. In the chapter of *Families at the Crossroads* titled "The Superiority of Singleness," author Rodney Clapp challenges us to consider the unique freedoms of singleness (see Matthew 19 and 1 Corinthians 7) as well as the prophetic nature of being able to be content in God in all situations, including singleness. He writes that "a right understanding and practice of singleness is crucial to the health of Christian family." The freedoms of time, relationship and focus that Paul and Jesus enjoyed are a gift for some of us in order that we might grow and give to the work of the kingdom more effectively. Unfortunately, this is a biblical reality that is usually not considered or affirmed in most Asian church contexts.

Most people, however, do get married at some point. Yet the key here is not merely to hang on until that magic moment, but rather to interact with God over our life situations. How is God leading you to make the most use of your life right now?

For many Asian cultures, marriage, rather than college or turning eighteen, is the sign of adulthood. It is tempting, especially for Asian American women, to cease in one's development as a person or as an adult until the time of marriage. This is not wise. For Christians the call and presence of Jesus—not necessarily a spouse—should be our ticket to maturity and responsibility. What would the world be like if the apostle Paul or John Stott or Mother Teresa had decided that they needed to wait for their "other half" in order to start taking themselves seriously as an adult and make the most of their lives?

Those who want to grow as Christians should do so, as much as possible, whatever life situation they are in. To one friend in her thirties, purchasing a couch for herself was a big step toward deciding to be an adult, although she was not married. "I realized that I was waiting for a husband in order to move on with life," she told me. "God may not be giving me a husband right now, but he certainly is wanting me to grow—and grow up!"

God may or may not honor our cultural social clocks. He may lead some of us into marriage at a time in our lives that matches cultural expectations. For some this will not be true. We can't control our family's or our church's response, but we can control our own. As we struggle to keep our identity safely in Jesus alone, he promises us comfort, direction and fruitfulness in whatever life situation he brings us.

Competing Views of Marriage

When my (Peter's) family immigrated to the United States in 1972, one of our favorite TV shows was *The Brady Bunch*. We were drawn to the show every Friday evening partly because it allowed us to see an American family in action, an American marriage at work. In the Brady family, Mom and Dad always talked to one another (but never fought), solved family "crises" together, and hugged and kissed each other all the time. Mike and Carol Brady were presented as best friends, romantic lovers and terrific partners in parenting. For us a part of being Americanized meant daydreaming about finding such a spouse and enjoying such a marriage relationship.

Around the same time, as I was entering my early adolescent years, my father began to talk to me about what marriage is and what kind of a spouse I needed to look for. My father was a man of few words, a stoic Asian father. But on the topic of marriage he had a lot to say. I think his reasoning was that if his oldest son (me) would go on the right path of marriage, the rest of his children would not go astray. He therefore persistently instructed me on this topic and let me know what kind of a woman should come into our family as the first daughter-in-law.

As a pastor, he insisted that I marry a person who came from a respectable Christian family, preferably a daughter of a respected pastor or an elder of a church (like many other Asian parents, he assumed that a fine Christian home only can produce a fine Christian young man or woman). He also wanted a daughter-in-law who came from a proper family (read: traditional Korean family) in which she had received first-rate "family education"—that is, she had properly learned the cultural norms and mores that would enable her to be a model wife and mother and, yes, a daughter-in-law who would be willing and able to take care of my aging parents. So the list went on.

Conspicuously absent from his list, however, was that the woman should be someone I would be in love with, someone I would regard as my best friend, my soul mate. The picture of marriage my father was portraying to me was quite different from the "American" marriage I was observing with a good deal of interest.

In many Asian cultures marriage has been perceived primarily as a social contract between two individuals, between two families. Marriage is based on and maintained largely by a sense of duty—a duty such as producing male heirs and providing for the children. In such a relationship the emphasis is not on romantic love. In fact, even if there are some sparks of romance in a marital relationship, these feelings are often suppressed, because in Confucian society the repressing of one's emotions is regarded as a sign of culture and education.

Furthermore, a traditional Asian marriage is a social contract that highlights the different roles husbands and wives play; it often functions like a performance contract. Typically, "inside the home" is considered the wife's domain, whereas that of the husband is "outside the home." (A commonly used term for "wife" in Korean is *an-saram*, and in Japanese *okusan*, which literally mean "inside person.")

What is distinctive here is not so much that there is an inside/outside home division of labor by sex, but the rigidity of this division, which discourages any crossovers, particularly men entering the "inside the home" domain. I have a Korean American friend who is a wonderful Mr. Mom. Since his wife works full time, he does a lot of house chores. When his mother visits them, however, against his wishes my friend refrains from all domestic duties, because that would put his wife in a bad light with his mother.

Although these inside/outside home domains in an Asian marriage can be viewed as complementary, they are not viewed as equal. The wife may be mistress of her own sphere, but since the husband is master of the outside sphere, which encompasses the inside sphere, she must follow in the direction in which he leads the entire family. Add to this the Confucian view of woman (see chapter seven), and there is an undeniable quality of male dominance in a traditional Asian marriage. A well-known Korean proverb advises women about how to adjust to married life: "Blind for three years, deaf for three years, mute for three years." This instruction clearly calls for the self-renunciation of wives, encouraging them to respond contrarily to what their husbands deem fit.

For many of us who grew up in North America, a traditional Asian marriage is quite unappealing; it seems emotionally ungratifying, rigid and even oppressive. So, in a reactionary spirit, we tend to romanticize the white, middle-class, American model of marriage. The alarmingly high rate of divorce in the United States, however, points to the fact that this type of marriage has a dark side too. For one thing, because it is a relationship that runs on love, it is greatly affected by fluctuations of a couple's emotions. There is a deep sense of uncertainty and precariousness, because nothing is given. If and when the content of either or both spouses' emotions wanes, the quality of a marriage suffers, and what results is divorce, a tragic breakup of a family. The Western type of marriage lacks the sense of stability and permanence that traditional Asian marriage offers.

As bicultural individuals, we often talk about enjoying the best of both worlds. When I listen to my Asian American friends talk about an ideal marriage, I think what they strongly desire is to create an "Asian American" marriage that brings together the best elements of the Asian and American marriage types. We want a marriage relationship that will last—a marriage that is founded on lifelong commitment to one another, reinforced by the stabilizing force of ethical duty. At the same time, we also want to enjoy a marriage relationship that offers a mutually satisfying sense of love, fulfilling each other's needs and desires for intimacy and affection. Are we asking for too much? I want to suggest that such a view of marriage is neither unrealistic nor new—the Bible has been teaching it for centuries.

The Biblical View of Marriage

According to the Bible, marriage is neither a private action of two persons in love nor simply a binding legal and social contract. Rather, marriage is portrayed as a covenantal relationship (Proverbs 2:17; Malachi 2:14). As God and the people of Israel have exchanged the vows of permanent and exclusive loyalty to one another—"you shall be my people, and I will be your God" (see Exodus 19:8; Deuteronomy 10:12-22; Jeremiah 30:22)—husband and wife are to commit to one another for life.

In a sense the word *covenant* includes the idea of contract. Like the Asian concept of marriage, it calls for an exclusive and long-lasting commitment. As God has loved his people faithfully and in a long-suffering manner, so married couples are to love one another persistently and exclusively.

At the same time, however, a covenant is far more than a treaty that mandates certain obligations and duties between two parties. The essence of covenant in the Bible also emphasizes a dynamic, loving relationship. God has expressed and continues to express his love for his people creatively, tenderly and sacrificially; he speaks many different "languages of love" to his people, so that no matter where they are in their life experiences, history or culture, they clearly experience his deep love for them. In like manner married couples are to learn to love one another—learning to provide for one another emotional support, intellectual stimulation, sexual satisfaction and spiritual companionship.

Finally, marriage as a covenant also has a political dimension; that is, it involves an issue of power. Recently the church has been debating the issue of the headship of the man/husband with much vigor. But what does such headship look like in everyday life? Growing up in a Korean American church, I was taught that the headship of a husband meant authority and ruling over his wife, a teaching that only reinforced the hierarchy of marriage roles created and sustained by the Confucian culture. When Ephesians 5:21-33 was taught or preached, the main focus was on verses 22-24 ("wives, be subject to your husbands as you are to the Lord"); a submissive wife was seen as the key ingredient of a godly marriage and Christ-honoring family life.

Later, during my seminary years, I learned that the passage does not teach the unilateral submission of wives. In fact, I learned that the revolutionary impact of the passage lies on its insistence that spouses submit to one another "out of reverence for Christ" (Ephesians 5:21). The passage is calling the husband to exercise the headship of being the servant leader of the family, as Jesus modeled for the church (Ephesians 5:25). Headship, in the context of servant leadership, emphasizes the greater *responsibility*—not the greater power—the husband has in caring for the wife.

A Christ-centered covenantal relationship calls for a quality of mutuality and reciprocity in marriage. It challenges husbands to love their wives selflessly and sacrificially; it exhorts wives to honor and respect their husbands. Such a relationship is characterized by neither male dominance nor rigid division of labor by gender. Rather, it should be characterized by self-giving love and service that motivate spouses to "fight for the bottom of the pile." What a radical idea!

The Pathway to a Healthy Marriage

In any culture, building a Christ-centered marriage will require hard work, because the project inevitably calls for countercultural attitudes, values and actions. For Asian American couples, given the strong patriarchal nature of our Confucian-based culture, living out the principle of mutual submission is one of the most challenging tasks to learn for husbands as well as for wives.

When my wife, Phyllis, and I met seventeen years ago as college students, she quickly labeled me an ethnocentric male chauvinist, and I returned the favor by calling her a hard-core "banana" feminist. Although we both grew up in Korean families, culturally speaking we were on opposite ends of the spectrum. During the early phase of our dating years, we were constantly arguing over the merits of the traditional Asian model of marriage; I vigorously defended the model, and Phyllis, with an equal amount of enthusiasm, sought to debunk it. Given this starting point, God had much to teach both of us about mutual submission.

The main lesson God has taught me during our twelve years of marriage is servant leadership at home. Having grown up as the first-born Asian son, pampered by mother and three sisters all along, I did not find it easy or natural to serve my wife at home by learning to cook, doing the laundry and caring for our young children. Especially during Phyllis's vocational training years, when the majority of the domestic chores fell in my lap, I felt I had two choices: either struggle in the pit of resentment and self-pity or welcome the opportunity to grow as a servant leader of the family, learning to love my wife as Christ loved the church.

Another expression of my servant leadership at home called for the readjustment of my vocational goals. When God gave us Nathaniel and Elaine while Phyllis was still in her rigorous training years, I had to step in and be the primary parent. I worked fewer hours, limited my ministry duties and turned down many ministry offers. While more and more of my seminary friends were being installed as senior pastors of churches of all sizes, I was struggling with my new role as a Mr. Mom.

I am grateful that through our marriage, God has taught me an invaluable lesson on servanthood. I am convinced that my growth in servant leadership at home deeply affects my servant leadership at my church and in other public ministry settings. I am also glad that my marriage has taught me to travel between the "inside/outside home" domains with ease and even joy. I count it a deep privilege that I am among few fathers who have been able to spend a lot of time with their young children. Finally, I am hopeful that if and when my now six-year-old son decides to get married, having grown up with Mr. Mom-Dad, he will be at a much better place to start the journey of being a servant leader in a new family.

For my wife, Phyllis, the main challenge was to learn to love and respect a Korean man. On our first date Phyllis honestly confessed to me that she always imagined she would marry a white guy because she thought Korean men were rude and chauvinistic (my insensitive, ethnocentric remarks further confirmed her suspicions). It was also evident that she greatly resented some aspects of Korean culture. "Why did my younger brother receive the royal treatment?" asked Phyllis. She identified herself as a feminist not because she carefully had thought through the philosophical agendas of the movement but because she was reacting strongly against many patriarchal aspects of the Korean culture.

Phyllis disliked Korean men, particularly their condescending attitude toward women; she disliked Korean culture even more, for encouraging and legitimating such attitudes in our families and even in our churches. So for her, dating and then marrying a "1.5-generation" Korean man was itself an act of faith. For her, learning to trust and to respect a Korean American husband was not a simple task, because it required her to process constructively many negative feelings she had toward Korean culture and Korean men and because it required a faith and hope that in God's grace we could build a new type of marriage and family.

Seventeen years after we first met, Phyllis and I are at a very different place as an Asian American man and woman, as a husband and a wife, as two disciples of Christ. Although we have frequently failed at and continuously struggle with the principle of mutual submission, having this principle as one of the main goals of our marriage has helped us to renounce those cultural mores that are unbiblical and unjust, as well as affirm biblical and cultural principles that can serve as important building blocks of healthy marriage.

Finding That Right Person—Asian American Style

Most of our Asian ancestors never worried about finding that right person to marry. They did not have to. In a traditional Asian setting, marriage was customarily arranged by fathers. A child had absolutely no voice in choosing his or her spouse; in many cases potential spouses never even saw each other's faces until the wedding night.

Thanks to modernization and globalization, most Asian countries have adopted some form of dating as a part of the spouse-selecting process. It seems that most of our parents, compared with their parents, exercised a greater amount of freedom in finding their spouses. The unspoken rule that everyone understood clearly, however, was that the parents had the last word.

In most cases our parents want to maintain a similar kind of balance; they don't mind our meeting and dating individuals of our choice, but they want to reserve the right to approve or disapprove the person we choose. Many of us would interpret this as a rude intrusion into our private lives, prompted by either our parents' lack of trust in our own judgment or their desire to control our lives. In most cases, however, our parents' participation in our marriage process is motivated by some important cultural values.

For Asian parents, finding a spouse for their sons and daughters is the final obligation they have as parents. As the oldest son, I have been asking my widowed mother to sell her home in northern Virginia and come live with us. She has been very reluctant thus far. Her main reason is that three of my younger siblings who live in that area are still single. She feels deeply that her last duty as a parent is to care for them and help them find the right partners. For most of our parents, parental duty did not end when they sent us off to college.

Another reason our parents feel deeply about getting involved in our marriage process is that to them the act of marriage is the uniting of two families, not just two individuals. They feel it is their responsibility to find out what the other family is like. So when Phyllis and I became engaged, I, following our parents' wishes, did not surprise her with the ring at a romantic restaurant or standing before the beautiful shoreline of Lake Michigan. Our engagement took place in her parents' family room, with many of our family members present. As a part of the ceremony, after declaring that we were engaged to be married, we made ceremonial deep bows to our parents and to her grandmother. Our engagement ceremony declared not only Phyllis's and my intent to be married but also that the two families were entering into a new family relationship with one another.

Our family's involvement can be very helpful, for they bring many insights and much wisdom from their life experiences. What happens, however, when their wishes clash with ours? What should we do when their demands are simply wrong or unbiblical? I have known some Asian American dating couples who were struggling. Their parents opposed their upcoming marriages because one person came from a family that belonged to a different socioeconomic class, a different ethnic group—and sometimes because the woman was a few years older than the man. None of these reasons can be supported by biblical principles. Before dismissing our parents' opposition as cultural gibberish and moving on with our wedding plans, however, we need to pause and think about the implication of the biblical command to honor our parents in this context.

Initially my father opposed my dating Phyllis. "Phyllis seems like a nice person, but you should not marry her," said my father one day, clearly concerned. When I asked why, he simply replied, "Because she wants to become a physician and because she does not speak Korean.

"Since God has called you to full-time ministry," my father reasoned, "you need to marry a person who is willing to serve as a full-time pastor's wife. Besides, if you plan to serve in a Korean church, your wife had better be able to speak the Korean language."

I heard my father's concerns and continually talked with him about Phyllis's and my future life plans and ministry plans. Phyllis also brushed up on her Korean and made valiant efforts to speak to him in the Korean language, often with comical results. Five years later, with my father's blessing, we were married, and it was a very rewarding thing for me to see that the relationship between my father and my newlywed wife was blossoming into a warm and fun father-daughter relationship.

Our desire to honor our parents does not always lead to a happy ending. However, making an earnest effort to honor our parents—especially when we disagree with them—is an act that honors our God (Ruth 1:15-18). We cannot be responsible for the final outcome; we trust the Lord with that. But it is our responsibility not to exclude our parents from the process too prematurely or in a dishonoring manner. Especially because Asian parents continue to play a significant role in our married lives, demonstrating attitudes of love and honor toward them during our courtship years is particularly important for us.

Interracial Dating and Marriage: "One Billion Chinese and She Can't Choose One!"

Seven years ago I (Susan) was driving with my mother and a friend to have a nice dinner at a Korean restaurant. "So if you marry anyone other than a Korean," my mother concluded her reflections on the topic of marriage, "I will not go to your wedding." Mom had no idea at that time that my friend was dating a Caucasian—or that I would marry a Caucasian seven years later.

Interracial dating is often a major tension point in being an Asian American today. For some of our parents it feels viscerally wrong, dishonoring of our cultures, and even contrary to God's plan. The father of one young woman who had begun seriously dating a non-Asian complained to his family, "One billion Chinese in the world and she can't choose one!"

The outmarriage rates of Asian women create tensions among Asian men, who end up feeling, *Hey! What's wrong with us that so many of our women are choosing non-Asian men?* Tension also exists in churches and other cultural hub centers where there is much pressure to be seen with "the right" (read: Asian) partner.

I find it comforting to know that Moses also encountered this tension as he married outside of his ethnic group. Numbers 12 tells of his brother and sister's racism and nonacceptance of his Cushite wife (Cush was in northeastern Africa or Ethiopia). God clearly sided with Moses in his decision to marry crossculturally, and God publicly validated him as one who could discern the will of God. Miriam was punished with temporary leprosy for her chastisement of her brother.

Peter Cha's reflections on the purpose of marriage are helpful in considering crossethnic marriages. The central biblical principles have to do with being partners in the journey of faith. The most important criterion is that the person be helpful to you in living a life of trusting God. This *can* be done crossculturally.

There are also many unique blessings to crosscultural relationships, such as constantly being forced to be a learner and to be stretched culturally. I suspect that as this country, and especially the urban context, becomes more diverse and racially intertwined, crossethnic couples will have certain inroads for serving and being heard in culturally sensitive situations. Doug, a Caucasian friend of mine, sensed God's leading for him to join and minister in an African-American church. Having worked through many issues with his Asian wife, Sandy, gave him sensitivity and integrity as he entered into a potentially difficult context.

Yet it is important not to be naive or irresponsible about the costs that must be counted and paid in entering into a crosscultural relationship. It is not an easy path. My aunt, who married a Caucasian man, was well aware of the difficulties her family would have to face as she married Uncle John. She remembers my Grandmother Cho, a very outspoken and intelligent woman, telling her, "If you marry this man, you effectively make a deaf mute out of me, because I will not be able to communicate with him or his family."

Communication is a big reason many parents hope their children do not marry outside of the culture. The challenge involves not only actual language barriers but also the more subtle, nonverbal ways of communicating. One friend's mother wondered why her daughter's boyfriend laughed and smiled so much around her. Her assumption was that he didn't want to treat her as a serious and honorable person, when he was actually just trying to be friendly.

As I entered into a crosscultural marriage with Alex, we spent much time considering and counting the various costs of my being Korean American and his being Dutch-German-Irish American. We have talked to many of our biracial friends and thought about the difficulties of having kids who are between worlds. We have spent lots of time talking about the prejudices we have concerning each other's community. We have had to work extra hard to connect with each other's parents. (Alex has done a great job!)

It is easy to fall in love with someone. It is harder to be wise about what having vastly different backgrounds can mean. Marriage brings up myriad deeper communication issues. I sometimes think that I am being totally clear through my nonverbal cues. Alex expects that if I want something, I should say so. This dynamic has led to some painful realizations of the ways that we are different. We expect that as our marriage grows, we will continue to put much time and effort into honoring and understanding the cultural backgrounds that we bring into the relationship.

Making It Work

If you are considering a crosscultural dating or marriage relationship, consider Jesus' advice to his followers in Luke 14:28-32 (count the cost). Know as much as you can, ahead of time, what the cost of making such a choice will be. Are you really prepared to pay that cost maturely?

For those who answer yes in faith, humility and out of a sense of call, here are some practical suggestions.

□ *Value and honor each other's family traditions and cultures as much as you can.* This will make things easier by helping your parents to sense your willingness to stretch to meet them. Alex will eat *anything* that is Korean or that my mother makes. I have taken a great interest in North Dakota farm culture, where Alex's grandparents came from.

☐ *Spend quality time with each other's parents and family.* This might be easy to avoid because of the discomfort, yet your family is the most important resource in getting to know your culture.

☐ *Be aware that one of your cultures may get much more airtime in your relationship.* Be sensitive to give space to both your backgrounds so that one of you doesn't end up feeling lost or not understood later. Because Alex and I live and minister in a predominantly white culture, we put out extra effort to keep up with what is going on in the Korean community, and we hang out in Koreatown and with Korean friends.

☐ *Know that there are some things that your partner may not be able to understand or connect with very fully in your journey of faith and cultural self-understanding.* When a Filipino American friend of mine went through a long process of coming to accept himself as an Asian, his Caucasian wife could sympathize—but not empathize. There were certain parts of the journey that he just had to travel alone.

As you might have guessed, my mother did decide to change her mind and come to (and bless) my wedding to Alex, a very non-Asian man. Through the grace of God she was able to accept him as a God-given son and good Christian partner for me. I am sure that it wasn't easy for her, and it's not easy for all those parents out there who want their kids just to have a nice, normal life. Yet this risk of faith has been a tremendously wonderful one for me and for my family. May Jesus give great graciousness and patience to all those who are struggling with similar situations.

Keep Talking

Dating, sex and marriage are relevant issues for all of us. But for Asian Americans, these topics are even more inviting and intriguing because they are rarely brought up in our family or church settings. It is often around these areas that the most contested bicultural conflicts and disagreements arise. We hope this chapter stimulates open and honest discussions around the issues of marriage and singleness and what the Bible says about these matters. We pray that you will find God's will for yourself—whether married or single.

7 The Gender Trap

Peter Cha &
Jeanette Yep

Looking around at the sisters and girl cousins eating,
great grandfather shouts, "Maggots!
Where are my grandsons? I want grandsons!"
MAXINE HONG KINGSTON, The Woman Warrior

"THE LAST GIRL" WAS THE LITERAL MEANING OF MY (PETER) FRIEND'S unusual Korean name. She was the third daughter of a Korean American family, and her parents so strongly wished that she would be their last daughter, and were so disappointed that she was a girl, that they gave her that odd name.

It is a tragedy to have a name that denies who you are. I wonder how my friend felt growing up, thousands of times hearing and responding to the name that reminded her that she was supposed to be a boy, that she was a mistake.

Men also face difficult issues. Often the media depict Asian American men as passive and asexual, brilliant technowizards or kung-fu stars who can decimate an entire brigade with quick kicks and deft blows. Sports broadcasters and writers still seem a little befuddled when they report on Michael Chang's nationality as he competes as the number-two seeded tennis player in the world.

The thrust for a long time has been to feminize Asian men. . . . I felt like I had to overcompensate, to prove that I could be assertive and play sports and be a ladies' man. (Andrew, *A. Magazine,* February/March 1997)

What's important for our future is our representation in the media. Having more [Asian men] in that scene. People seeing Asian men as normal and attractive is extremely important. We have to force ourselves not to accept the passivity we've been accustomed to. (Steve, *A. Magazine,* February/March 1997)

Discovering Who We Are

It's tough to know what it means to be a woman or man these days. There are lots of voices. Some we choose to tune in to, allowing them to influence us as we attempt to construct our identity as a man or woman. Other voices can be more subtle—their messages are almost subliminal. Most of the time we do not choose to examine critically the cacophony of voices and messages we have received and assimilated into our personhood over our lifetime. And, despite wanting to be biblically based Christians, seldom do we evaluate these voices in light of God's Word. What's the result? In the body of Christ there's sometimes confusion, fear and misunderstanding on the part of women and men, leading to an uncritical business-as-usual attitude when it comes to gender.

Think of the issues that contribute to our view of gender as elements of an orchestra. The brass section is perhaps the loudest section, helping define who we are as men and women. It is the postmodern North American dominant culture. These horn sections clearly and loudly play out perceptions and definitions of gender that we can't help but listen to. In popular culture we come face to face with androgyny, sexual identity confusion, the gay-lesbian lifestyle and Calvin Klein advertisements. Comedian Ellen DeGeneres comes out of the closet in prime time while forty-two million American households watch. Dennis Rodman dresses in a white bridal gown yet plays in the quintessence-of-macho basketball world of the NBA. We are left to wonder, *Who's who and what's what?*

While I (Jeanette) was growing up, the hippie era was in full bloom.

Free love. Make love not war. Bell bottoms. Unisex clothing. Long hair for men and women. When we drove around in the Yepmobile in that era, my immigrant mother would not infrequently point at someone and say, loudly, in our Chinese dialect, "This one—is it a boy or a girl?"

I'd roll my eyes and squirm, grateful that most of the folks in the world didn't speak our dialect! But inside I'd be wondering too, *Yeah, is he/she a boy or a girl?*

The wind section also plays in this orchestra. Less obtrusive than the brass section, the woodwinds provide a depth of sound and a variety of tones. Perhaps it's analogous to the role of the conservative church culture many of us have experienced. Like the dominant culture, the church offers a set of definitions of what it means to be a Christian man or woman. Well-meaning and sincere Christians who affirm the authority of Scripture come to different conclusions about gender roles, as well as about leadership in the home and in the church. The debate between the camps can be strong, forceful and, at times, emotional. What's a Christian man or woman to do? The notes played can sound dissonant at times. Theologians on both sides of the issue argue forcefully and convincingly, espousing their "correct" and biblical interpretation of womanhood and manhood. Those of us who are laypeople may wonder, *Who am I, a lay believer, to judge? Can somebody tell me what and how to think about this topic?*

A third section in our orchestra is the strings section, which represents traditional Asian culture and is foundational to an orchestra. Sometimes the string section plays a quiet theme that may go unnoticed. It may even seem subliminal. But an orchestral performance can't go on without its string section. In other words, there is a Confucian foundation underneath the values and social structure of our Asian American families. Because it is "us," this foundation can go unexamined. And Confucius was big on hierarchy and male leadership.

Putting all these sections together—the brass, the woodwinds and the strings (our dominant North American culture, our conservative church culture and our family's Confucian basis)—Asian American Christians listen to an orchestra where each section is playing its part of the score. All these sections contribute to the concerto we hear that forms our self-perceptions. Sometimes the sections in the orchestra blend to make music that lifts our souls. Other times each section plays its portion of the score, only to produce a painfully dissonant and confusing cacophony. In any case, playing in harmony takes lots of practice—as individuals, as a section and as an entire orchestra. No wonder it's tough to figure out what it means to be a Christian man or woman!

As you've listened to the orchestra playing the music that tells us about gender, have you ever wished that you were of the other gender? Have you ever thought that the other gender gets the better end of the deal when it comes to parental and family expectations, acceptance in mainstream culture and opportunities in the church? I confess that at times I have. I've wished more than once that I was born a son and not a daughter.

Confucius Say ...

In my (Jeanette's) family, Confucius said loudly and clearly, "It's a man's world." My parents had four children. The first three were daughters and the fourth a son, the male heir. Hooray! The dynasty could continue! Recently my mother matter-of-factly recounted that my brother received more "hung-baos" (cash gifts placed in red envelopes) at his birth than any of the daughters. I didn't need to ask why. I knew the answer: "Because he's a boy."

Growing up, I observed that our relatives seemed more concerned for his welfare, health and educational achievements than for ours. Going against the grain, my parents worked hard at treating each child equally. And I relished being the captain of the "equity squad," reminding my parents of any perceived or actual injustice. But despite their attempts, I knew that boys in general, and my brother specifically, got the better end of the deal. Boys got more freedom to come and go as they pleased, and more familial favor (especially from the extended family). More expectations also were part of the deal, but it seemed to me that the perks outweighed the expectations.

In subtle and overt ways, I learned that a "quiverful" of boys was an incredible blessing from God. And having a quiverful of girls was a hardship to be endured. Seeing this Chinese family dynamic, was it any coincidence that I often wished I were a boy?

The Confucian Legacy

A wise rabbi once said, "Those who are not proud to be heirs are not fit to be pioneers." As an Asian American, I (Peter) gratefully acknowledge many wonderful legacies we have received from our forebears, but our cultural view of gender is not one of them. Regretfully, our Confucian-based cultures forcefully and consistently taught that women are categorically inferior and that they are to exist as "nameless" individuals whose primary—if not only—purpose is to give birth to sons and to serve their men.

The lingering effects of these traditional teachings and practices continue to shape our lives and identities today.

From its very early years, Confucianism assumed that the hierarchical relationship between men and women was an important ethical mandate with which no one should tinker. One of the important Confucian principles, the principle of the Three Bonds, teaches that "the ruler, the father, and the husband are to be the standards of the ruled, the son, and the wife" (Wing-Tsit Chan, *Source Book in Chinese Philosophy*). In these three vertical relationships, the superior partners were called "masters." They were given control over their inferior partners. Along with other teachings, this principle formalized and intensified the relationship of dominance-submission between ruler and ruled, between parents and children, and between husbands and wives.

The principle of the Three Obediences was another important Confucian principle that played a significant role in shaping the lives and experiences of women. It taught that all women are to obey fathers when unmarried, husbands when married, and sons when widowed! Women are to submit not only to their fathers and husbands, but, when widowed, also to their sons. Not just wives' full submission to their husbands but also women's categorical subordination to men became a powerful and rigid norm in many Asian cultures, sanctioned and legitimated by the full weight of the Confucian worldview and way of life.

In such a society a woman did not have her own identity as a person. Just before my father died, I was talking to him about his family members who were left behind in North Korea. When we were talking about my grandmother, I found out that my father did not know her name. "How can you not know your own mother's name? Did she not have a name?" I asked in disbelief. He said that the people in his family and village referred to her as a woman from the Song family. That was the common practice then, he said.

In traditional Korean society women were called "so-and-so's" daughter before marriage, "so-and-so's" wife after marriage and "so-and-so's" mother after a child's (son's) birth. These women were nameless because they did not have identities of their own. Their sense of being was very much wrapped up in the roles they played for others, particularly for the men in their lives. In many ways women were seen and treated as possessions, even as recently as the beginning of this century.

My grandmother was addressed by her maiden name. Traditionally Asian women did not take their husbands' last names, for they did not count as a member of the man's family. In America the practice of keeping one's maiden name is seen as a woman's independent identity; in Asia it's a sign of a woman's *non*identity.

Because home was the only proper place for women, their activities in the public arena were severely restricted. In the Confucian Korea, a woman's appearance in public was legally prohibited; women were permitted to go outside their homes only during the night (from 9:00 p.m. to 2:00 a.m.). These restrictions effectively prohibited women from working or performing activities outside the home, especially since violations of these rules could result in the punishment of receiving eighty lashes in public (Kim, *Women of Korea*).

Finally, a Confucian society is a patrilineal society, which dictates that only sons can carry out the family name and tradition. Daughters, according to an ancient Korean saying, are "strangers after leaving natal home." It is no wonder that every parent wanted to have sons but not daughters. This attitude of strong preference for sons is still alive and well in many Asian settings. Thousands of Chinese parents' "dumping" their daughters as a response to China's one-child policy constitutes a tragic modern example of these ancient mores at work.

We may never have heard of the principles of the Three Bonds or the Three Obediences. Nevertheless, we must not underestimate the cumulative effects of centuries of teaching and practices. To continue our lives as if there is nothing wrong with the gender relationships in our home, church and community is to sanction and approve the ongoing tradition of mistreating and dehumanizing women in our culture.

Men in the Trap

Men face other issues in this postmodern, Christian, Confucian, Asian American gender trap. The church doesn't seem to have a well-defined place or even a category for Asian American male leadership yet. (With the notable exception of the recently formed "Asian Promise Keepers"—a subsection of the parent national men's ministry known as Promise Keepers.) Often men don't have much voice in their vocational choices because of family and cultural expectations and the pressure of carrying on the family name, of preserving the dynasty.

Once I (Jeanette) was dining with some highly successful professional Asian Americans. We went around the table and shared what we did and what we wish we could have done, if there had been no obstacles, if we could have just followed our hearts. One person shared how he would have gone into elementary school teaching, but now he had been spoiled by his better-paying, prestigious finance job. Someone else said he would have become a movie critic—the Asian Roger Ebert. Another person wanted to be a carpenter. Someone else wanted to have become a gourmet chef.

I asked folks what prevented them from pursuing their vocational dreams. They answered, "It doesn't pay well enough." "I have younger brothers and sisters I have to support through college." "I never could have done that; it would have killed my parents."

It seemed to weigh more heavily on the men to fulfill their parents' career expectations of them. Most of the men didn't even allow themselves to dream of pursuing their heart's interest as a vocation. But interestingly enough, most of them had figured out how to pursue their "specialty" as a hobby. From our conversation that evening, it seemed that the wo-men were given more vocational latitude since they would marry and bear children someday. Even though the men a-round the dining table were successful and accomplished by society's standards, many still felt that they weren't good enough yet by their parents' standards. Treading with their heads above the surface was the best many could do in this gender game.

Women: "Be All That You Can Be"

I (Jeanette) attended a small, private Eastern women's college in the mid-seventies. Bras had been burned. The Equal Rights Amendment was introduced to Congress. Some women, and some men, were trying to right an inequity that paid women fifty-nine cents for every dollar a man earned for the same work. Sadly, it hasn't changed that much. The average U.S. woman working full time still makes only "71 cents for each dollar earned by a man," according to research done by the U.S.

Proud of Me—for Sons and Fathers
Ji Lim

I've tried all of my life
to be your boy
I cried all of the nights
when you would not hold me
and so, so I pretend
to feel nothing
I feel everything

Won't you please
be proud of me
when I can't be your boy
please be proud of me
when I can't fit your mold

I fought every right
every need to turn away
I thought it'd be alright
in time you would tell me

but now, now we've grown old
why do I hold
still dearly hold

Won't you please be proud of me
when I can't be your boy
please be proud of me
when I can't fit your mold

and so, so I pretend
to feel nothing
I feel everything

Bureau of the Census (Carol Kleiman, "Research on Equal Pay Should Earn Respect," *Chicago Tribune,* September 9, 1997). In the decades of the sixties and seventies in the U.S., men and women were asking some fundamental questions about gender and their roles in society, the family and the church.

As a Mount Holyoke woman, I clearly received the message that I could be a superwoman and have it all, which meant a fulfilling career, a loving husband, 2.5 children, my own home and a pet or two. I was told that the sky was the limit in terms of developing my potential as a woman. I was as ambitious and career-oriented as any of my classmates. And I loved the opportunities I had in a woman's college to try, to fail and to grow as a person both academically and socially.

As my spiritual commitment deepened in college, I reengaged the conservative Christian church's view of gender issues. I was shocked. Hurt. Angry. Lots of times I contemplated "tubing" my faith because of the second-class treatment received by gifted and equipped women in the church. There was such a tension, even a war, between the Mount Holyoke "you can have it all" side of me and the conservative, evangelical Christian/church culture side of me. It sure didn't feel like I could "be all that I could be" as a Christian woman, that was for sure!

Years later I was invited to teach a college-age Sunday-school class for my church on the inductive Bible study method. Things proceeded well for a time, until the ten-week quarter was nearly over. Then, after class one day, Tim, a graduate student member, came to me and said that I couldn't teach Sunday school anymore. He had chatted with the pastor and they agreed. Tim would be taking over, and he would finish out the quarter.

In shock, I asked why was I being pulled. He said it was because there were young men in the Sunday-school Bible study class. "The Bible doesn't allow you to teach young men—see 1 Timothy 2," Tim said with authority. So I was relieved of my duties midstream! I passed on my notes to Tim, and he finished teaching the quarter's curriculum.

That was painful. It probably could have been done better. And I probably could have responded differently. But the message to me was clear. As a woman, I would not be allowed to teach, preach or have any authority over men in the context of the ministry of that church. And up until today, many years later, that church has been consistent in upholding that biblical interpretation of gender roles.

Biblical Perspectives: Gender Equality and Mutual Submission

Critiquing our cultural view of gender must be grounded in the Bible. How does the Bible view men and women and the relationship between the two genders? The opening chapter of the Bible declares that man and woman were created equally in the image of God: "So God created humankind in his image, in the image of God he created them; male and female he created them" (Genesis 1:27). Furthermore, God blesses both Adam and Eve to be fruitful and exercise dominion over God's creation (1:28). It is clear that from the beginning, men and women were equal recipients both of the divine image and earthly rule. Both sexes were equally created by God and equally commissioned by him.

Then comes Genesis 3. As the result of sin entering into this world, not only was a deep sense of alienation introduced between human beings and God but also between the two sexes. Part of God's judgment on our disobedient ancestors was his word to the woman: "Your desire shall be for your husband, and he shall rule over you" (Genesis 3:16). In place of the equality of the one with the other, the domination of woman by man was introduced by the Fall.

Then in the fullness of time, Jesus came to reconcile us to God and to one another. Through his redemptive work on the cross, Christ created his new kingdom community in which, among other things, gender equality is reclaimed. Thus declared the apostle Paul in Galatians 3:28, "There is no longer Jew or Greek, there is no longer slave or free, there is no longer male and female; for all of you are one in Christ Jesus." In the Kingdom of God, one gender is not superior or inferior to the other. The gender equality, established by creation but perverted by the Fall, was recovered by the redemption that is in Jesus Christ. So, in God's new family, men and women are equally heirs of his grace in Christ (1 Peter 3:7).

This biblical truth fundamentally and radically challenges our cultural view of gender roles and status. How are we as Asian Americans, then, to think about this issue, particularly in light of our own culturally constructed gender ideology?

Four years ago, when three Asian American friends and I (Peter) began to dream about a new Asian American church in the Chicago area, one of the issues we discussed right away was the roles of women in the church. All of us agreed that most Asian immigrant churches fail to affirm and encourage our sisters. So the four of us (three of whom were seminary-trained Asian American men) prayerfully discussed starting an Asian American church that would biblically affirm all people of God, both men and women.

As a church, we decided that all members of the church should exercise their spiritual gifts regardless of race, age, socioeconomic background or gender. Since God created the New Testament church on the Day of Pentecost by pouring out his Holy Spirit on "all people," on his "slaves, both men and women" (Acts 2), we believe that we as a church have the stewardship responsibility of encouraging both men and women to discover and develop whatever spiritual gifts God may give them. Thus we have a number of gifted women who are serving the church as elders, as a worship leader and as a preacher/teacher. Their gracious and effective exercise of leadership has provided us not only with godly modeling but also with healing for many women and men in our Asian American congregation.

Also, we decided as a church to emphasize the concept of team ministry, the plurality of leadership. This emphasis has minimized the controversy over women's roles in the church. In the spirit of team ministry, the pastoral staff team serves alongside lay leaders—three of whom are women—to provide pastoral oversight. This plurality of leadership has encouraged men and women in the church to serve alongside one another with an attitude of mutual respect.

Finally, we seek to teach and model servant leadership at our church. The Bible, it seems to me, paradoxically teaches both gender equality and male headship, and that both of these biblical principles should be honored. Gender equality does not mean that men and women are the same, that they are identical. Furthermore, as men exercise a certain kind of leadership at home and at church, this leadership is to be characterized by sacrificial love, as modeled by our Lord Jesus Christ.

One of the critical mistakes Asian American Christians easily make is uncritically importing our culture's understanding of authority and submission and applying it to our family and church life. Let's face it: we come from a very hierarchy-oriented culture that views authority in terms of exercising power and control, and submission as unquestioning loyalty and obedience. Sadly, this view of authority prevails in many of our Asian churches and homes, making them vulnerable to all types of abuses, including abuses against and mistreatment of women.

Christ had a very radical idea about authority and submission. In Matthew 20:25-28, Jesus instructed that Christian leaders must not lord it over others and have authority over them. Rather, leaders should be servants. Authority and servant leadership are synonymous in God's kingdom! What does this mean in church life? For our church this means our pastors and lay leaders serve in the church nursery on certain Sunday mornings, and this also means men as well as women participate in preparing our church's monthly fellowship meals.

Similarly, husbands are referred to as "head" in Ephesians 5 because they are called to be servant leaders; they are to give themselves for their wives in love as Christ gave himself for the church. Once again, a husband's headship is not to be equated with lordship. Rather, it emphasizes the greater responsibility the husband has in caring for his wife. This biblical principle is not an easy thing to practice for many Asian American men, because our traditional culture has taught us all along that men are masters who are to lord it over their wives and that wives are the ones who have greater responsibility in caring for their spouses.

In this context of servant leadership, what does submission mean? The biblical view of submission emphasizes mutuality and reciprocity. It means, among other things, that men and women have the responsibility to teach one another humbly, to hold one another accountable before God, and to serve one another. In short, Christian submission does not call for servility or blind obedience. Rather, it calls for an attitude of mutual humility and of sacrificially caring about the interests of the other, for this is the attitude that Christ our Lord has modeled for us (Philippians 2:1-11).

Gender at Work

Christians in the work world face unique challenges as they try to be good stewards of their gifts. Asian Americans may not seem like managerial material to their superiors because they may not seem outwardly aggressive or boast enough about their accomplishments (see K. Connie Kang, "Chinese in the Southland: A Changing Picture," *Los Angeles Times,* June 29, 1997). Some women, especially those who are more diminutive in stature and are blessed with "youthful" genes, may have a hard time being taken seriously, as contributing more than just a "decorative" element to their work team. Some men may forever be seen as capable technocrats. (See chapter five for more on the bamboo ceiling.)

In my work in a Christian ministry, my (Jeanette's) manager and most of my colleagues are non-Asian. And despite my self-awareness about the dynamics of Asian and non-Asian cultures, I still have difficulty volunteering myself for projects (even when I know that I have something to contribute) or speaking up persistently enough to gain resources, recognition or the attention needed to accomplish a task.

The good news is that in contrast to the baby boomers who preceded them in the marketplace, some researchers have begun to note that twenty-something workers seem more intent on living a balanced life (so that their work doesn't define who they are). They also want to devote more time to their families. Women especially are expecting their employers to afford them the flexibility they need to raise children, including part-time jobs that won't cause long-term harm to their careers, just a temporary slowdown (see Pamela Kruger, "Superwoman's Daughters: They Don't Want Your Job," *Working Woman,* May 1994). The pendulum swings back; "being all that you can be" is being redefined by this generation of workers.

You go, girls (and boys)!

How Can We Get Free?

So you see, both men and women can become caught in the gender trap. The issues may be a bit different. Certainly there are individual family factors (like generation of immigration and socioeconomic level), and there are many exceptions to the rule, but Asian culture still favors boys over girls. And Christian Asian American women often face the double whammy of conservative theology and Confucian tradition. Asian men, on the other hand, are often marginalized in our society. At the same time, they bear incredible pressure to succeed and provide for their extended and nuclear families. All too often, we don't bother to examine prayerfully and critically the influence of culture in our understanding and interpretation of the Bible. However you look at it, the gender trap is painful. What's a man or woman to do?

I (Jeanette) am very hopeful for this generation of young adults. There is a great deal of potential, giftedness and skill among you. I love how you teach your elders the importance of community and friendships. And it's within the context of community that there is great hope for getting out of the gender trap. Here are some simple, practical strategies and suggestions.

☐ *Let's be quick to listen and hear before we move to correcting and amending our sisters' hurts and perceptions.* There can be great healing when we listen empathetically to one another. Kermit the Frog sang, "It's not easy being green," and for us the song might be, "It's not always easy being an Asian Christian woman."

☐ *Let's acknowledge the price men will (and do) pay as they attempt to live out a more biblical view of what it means to be male in a traditional Asian cultural framework.* Some will criticize men for being soft, emotional or feminine. Others will be critical of their partnership with their spouses—"Why don't you just tell your wife you're moving, if you have a good job offer elsewhere? Why are you worrying about her feelings so much? Don't you know the Korean saying, 'The thread must follow the needle'?" When our brothers are being put down, let's be quick to affirm, encourage and thank them for their countercultural leadership.

☐ *Let's recognize that there is a power dynamic in the relationship between men and women.* It's difficult for anyone in a power position to give up power. It's more comfortable to hang on to it. Asian men have been given the power in their relationship with women through Confucian culture, the dominant culture and the conservative church

Privileged Women?

"I feel that Asian women, in this society, are privileged above Asian men; there's a mainstream acceptance of Asian women in the media that men don't have. I feel that a lot of Asian women are not sensitive to that." (Greg, *A Magazine*)

culture. It is key for men to come to an awareness and understanding of the power dynamic in crossgender relationships. And women need to befriend men supportively and patiently as they journey and grow in their understanding of the role of power in relationships.

☐ *Let's affirm one another in the family and in the life of the church.* Men, get in the kitchen, help your mom (or wife) around the house, and show by your example and service that you love and honor your Christian sisters. Women, don't hide under a bushel your God-given gifts. Look for mentors. Seek out opportunities to be challenged, to grow and develop your gifts, even if they are the more traditionally male, up-front gifts of leadership and teaching. Let's be wise stewards of all the gifts God has given us.

☐ *Let's work at honest and open communication between the genders.* Not so much game playing. Be quicker to listen and ask questions than to answer and solve the problems of the other gender.

☐ *Let's form communities with like-minded friends who will support, encourage and pray for one another* as we listen to the many chords and melodies around us and try to bring them into harmony—as we attempt to discover the full meaning of being Christian Asian American women and men.

☐ *Let's encourage men to begin the process of increasing women's partnership in the ministry of the church.* As experts in persuasion theory point out, women don't have much "source credibility" in this discussion. But as brothers open doors in places and situations where women are not yet in full partnership, the change process can begin.

One man said to a friend, "This [biblical view of women in ministry] is essentially a nonissue for me." I think he meant well, but as a woman, I was hurt by his comment. How can he not speak up when men and women are still not able to fully serve the church with their God-given gifts and abilities? So men, take the lead in this area. Go ahead and make this your issue too!

Warning: It is vitally important that you personally examine the Scriptures and become fully persuaded about God's intention for men, women and his church. Only then will your motivation flow from a love for the truth of God's Word and not merely be a response to the (quickly changing) winds of culture.

☐ *And finally, let's be quick to acknowledge that learning to be Christian Asian American women and men is a lifelong journey and that we need each other as traveling companions.* Working together in mission, and serving alongside, crying with, listening to and caring for one another as Christian brothers and sisters is how community is formed. And as biblical communities are formed, witness will be one of the natural fruits of our life together. May the watching world see in us as individuals and in our healthy crossgender relationships the redemptive, grace-filled, hope-giving life of Christ.

8

Racial Reconciliation

Susan Cho Van Riesen & Peter Cha

Susan's Story

OUR CAMPUS FELLOWSHIP WAS HAVING AN END-OF-THE-YEAR SENIOR "roast and toast" banquet when a campus security officer came in and informed me that the neighborhood was burning. In response to Rodney King's arrest and beating, the city of Los Angeles, especially the area immediately surrounding the University of Southern California, had burst into chaos and rioting.

The students and I would not be allowed to go home that night. Instead, we all stayed in the dorm complex that we happened to be in. For the next twenty-four hours, we sang worship songs, held prayer meetings and ministered to people as we watched the city burn around us. Frightened students in the dorms who had never done anything Christian before knocked on the doors of Christian students and asked if they could pray for them. We watched the student resident advisors leave with no thought for the first-year and international students who had no cars or local contacts. We listened to Christian students call their parents and explain why they were staying in order to pray and serve.

I have never seen so much hope and hopelessness swirling around at the same time. Because our community had a vision for acting as agents of racial reconciliation, hundreds of students were organized to go out into the streets immediately and help out by sweeping, praying and driving mothers with no cars to buy groceries for their children (the grocery stores in their neighborhoods had all been burned down). Most of the students on the USC campus fled to nearby Orange County or flew home out of fear. Our students stayed out of faith. They invited frightened international students who had no place to go to pray with them, some of them for the first time. Students and staff from other fellowships in the area (UCLA and Occidental College) bought groceries and made huge pots of rice and beans so that we could feed people. It was an amazing time of the gospel being lived out.

God also left a lasting impression on my heart about how much alienation and distrust there is between the different ethnic groups in Los Angeles. Two days after the unrest began, my staff partner, Kevin Blue, and I drove around and witnessed an accident in Koreatown due to the absence of functioning street lights. When we offered ourselves as witnesses, we were fearfully and firmly asked to leave. As we drove away, I realized with shock that it was because I, a Korean American, was driving around with Kevin, an African-American. My people saw my brother as the enemy. The evil of people's hearts was being made manifest in the midst of the fear and chaos.

Peter's Story

While Susan found herself in the middle of the riots, I was closely following the news from Chicago. As a Korean American immigrant, I was deeply feeling the pain of fellow Korean Americans who were grieving over the loss of their possessions, their dreams and their hopes. I also felt their sense of fear, of feeling vulnerable and abandoned, as I watched Los Angeles Police Department patrol cars retreating from the Koreatown area. My immediate response was, *Why is this happening to my people, and how can this be happening in "mee-gook"* (a Korean word for America, which literally means "beautiful country")?

Watching the riots also brought back some of the memories of my earlier years in Los Angeles. I was twelve years old when our family immigrated to the U.S. Navigating through adolescence can be a trying and tricky task for anyone, but to do so in a setting where language and culture are totally strange to you is a special challenge. And adolescent kids can be so cruel to others, especially to those who are not like them. Almost daily I faced a variety of racial slurs and demeaning gestures. To make things worse, I had the misfortune of starting my immigrant life when David Carradine's *Kung Fu* TV drama was making its debut. As the kung fu craze swept through the country, including my primarily black school, I regularly encountered the question, "Hey man, do you know kung fu?" Often I was baited into a fight. I remember feeling very lonely, very helpless. Not knowing the language, I felt vulnerable and outnumbered. I often wondered why our family immigrated to this country, and I began to form my own hostile attitudes toward African-Americans in particular. Nearly twenty years later, it was not just the streets of Los Angeles that were experiencing a great deal of turmoil; I found myself confronting my own unresolved feelings of racial conflicts and prejudices.

A Vision for the Multicultural Kingdom of God: Susan

When I was a little girl, I used to ask my mother what heaven would be like.

"Will there be good food there? Will there be *Korean* food there?" (I couldn't imagine spending the rest of eternity without kimchee and rice.) I used to wonder if there were Korean churches in heaven, imagining that since that is the way we worshiped and knew God here on earth, that must be the way it was set up up there. I pictured St. Peter at the entrance to heaven directing people to the appropriate rooms with the appropriate food, music, language and so on: "Japanese? You go over there. Mexican? Right here, if you please. Watch your step."

Later, when I learned to allow the Bible, and not my imagination, to form my picture of heaven, I realized that my vision was too small. Revelation 7:9-12 sets a glorious scene of "a great multitude . . . from every nation, from all tribes and peoples and languages, standing before the throne and before the Lamb, robed in white, with palm branches in their hands. They cried out in a loud voice, saying,

'Salvation belongs to our God who is seated on the throne, and to the Lamb!' "

In this passage only two things are important: worshiping the Lamb and the inclusion of every group. Centuries of oppression, resentment, and pain will not get in the way of those who have made it to this sacred place. Language barriers, economic inequalities, and differing values and norms will not be an issue. Mistrust and the effects of miscommunication will have melted away. Think for a moment about how amazing this is! North Koreans and South Koreans, Japanese and Chinese, Germans and Jews, Serbs and Croats, all bending the knee and declaring the singular supreme worthiness of God. All of the differences will be fully transcended by the radiant glory of the Lamb of God, our Jesus!

To fully appreciate this picture, it is very important to understand that *each* group is there. The worshipers are not a gray, faceless blob or integrated into one dominant, supreme culture or ethnic group. Rather, the people of God form a beautiful mosaic or symphony, different voices and faces forming a unified diversity that perfectly gives glory to their one Savior. God will have redeemed not only individual people, but also cultures, so that they can stand in the presence of the Holy Lamb. We should be preparing to spend eternity together.

Yet if this is true, why is it that 11:00 a.m. on Sunday morning is still the most segregated hour in America? Given the images of the multicultural, gloriously diverse view of the final kingdom of God, one might expect that the church in America would be a light to society in this important arena. The gospel of Jesus has much to say about living justly, treating all people as children of God, and the freedom of love and reconciliation (Luke 10:29-37; John 4:1-26). The apostle Paul's letters are replete with teachings about the power of Jesus to bring believers together across great cultural divides (Galatians 2:11-14; 3:28; Ephesians 2:13-16). One of Peter's most dramatic personal lessons in his leadership involved being taught to minister and fellowship crossculturally (Acts 10:1—11:18). Yet the modern church, and especially Asian American churches, lag behind in terms of living and giving a vision of racial reconciliation in these troubled times.

Many Asian churches buy or build buildings in multiracial neighborhoods, yet few actively engage the neighborhood in which they are located with evangelism, justice ministries or relationship. Many committed young Asian leaders are being raised up, but few value or have the energy for crosscultural ministry. Some claim that exclusively homogeneous ministry is more efficient and, therefore, more effective. I must ask, however, since when is the gospel very efficient? Intercession, service, and laying down your life for the least seem very time inefficient, yet they are crucial elements of the way Jesus has asked us to minister. A reflection of our eternal destination—however imperfect—should be the goal of the community life of the church. There is much work to be done.

A Life-Changing Friendship: Susan

Earlier I mentioned driving around during the Los Angeles unrest of 1992 with my African-American staff partner, Kevin Blue. My relationship with Kevin has been one of the most profound graces in my life.

Kevin and I became friends as we led an outreach Bible study together during my junior year of college. It was an amazingly difficult beginning. Having grown up with mostly white and Korean friends in Eugene, Oregon, I found that everything about Kevin was different and uncomfortable for me. He spoke very directly and expected me to challenge him (three years my elder) to his face. We didn't understand each other's friends, sense of humor or food. Furthermore, I didn't understand what the big deal was about his sense that America was an unjust place. *Gee,* I'd think, *my parents were poor when they came, but they seemed to make it because of the opportunities this country offers. What's the big deal?* The big deal, of course, was the hundreds of years of the effects of slavery and social problems that I could not even begin to understand at that point in my life. Our conversations often were not pretty. It seemed impossible for us to be friends.

Yet an amazing thing happened for us as we gave ourselves to the ministry that God had set before us. We began to obey Jesus in his command to resolve conflict no matter how hard it was. We learned to be deeply honest with one another. We taught one another about our cultures and how we saw the kingdom of God through the unique lenses of our cultural experiences. Most important, we experienced, in living community, how much we had in common through our love for Jesus.

Kevin is now one of my dearest friends and a constant prophet and teacher to me in the power of the gospel to overcome barriers. He is no longer a "scary black man" to me, and I am not a "mousy Asian American woman" to him. Although we are now living in different communities and are involved in different ministries, our relationship continues to serve as a reminder of what God can do to bridge the gap between people.

A missionary in India once observed that many religions can duplicate signs and wonders, but only Jesus can command and bring deep reconciliation. We should seek to have living examples of this miraculous power of God in our lives. The relationships that believers have with each other—more than buildings, programs and sermons—are the most effective witness that we can have. What will seekers and non-Christians who are affected and burdened by the racial divides of this age see when they observe us? Are you willing to be a part of the living reflection of the coming reconciled kingdom of Jesus?

The Power of Repentance and Forgiveness: Peter

Several years ago at an InterVarsity regional conference, I was having lunch with some students from my chapter. Jeanette Yep, my InterVarsity supervisor, joined us and began to introduce herself to the students. When she found out that one of the students, Minh, was a Vietnamese American, Jeanette asked him, "Minh, when did you come to this country?"

Minh replied, "Sometime during the late seventies."

"Were you then one of the boat people?"

"Yes," said Minh.

Jeanette then stopped everything. Jeanette, a second-generation Chinese American woman, born and raised in Boston, said to this

Vietnamese student, "Minh, I want you to forgive my people for the wrongs that they have done to yours."

Listening to this conversation, I was very puzzled. Jeanette explained, "I've heard about the stories of Chinese boat owners, driven by sheer greed, exploiting the situation of the Vietnamese people wanting to get out of their country. I know that the Chinese would take their boats to Vietnam, load them with people beyond capacity and take them out into the China Sea, where many boats sank and many lives were lost." And so Jeanette asked for his forgiveness. Minh forgave.

What a powerful illustration of repentance, forgiveness and interethnic reconciliation. I shared this story at the Urbana 93 student mission convention, and God used it to start another ministry of reconciliation, this time between the Japanese and the Koreans. God used Jeanette and Minh's story particularly to challenge the Japanese delegates to repent publicly for the sins their nation had committed against the Koreans and to work toward reconciliation with Korean brothers and sisters.

During one of the morning sessions at an international student conference, which followed Urbana 93, all of the Japanese students stood and lined the walls of the auditorium as their leader expressed their repentance to Korean delegates. They then bowed to their knees with their faces to the floor before the audience! The next day, a spokesperson for the Korean delegates took the opportunity to acknowledge the Japanese expression of humility and love, and to express the Korean delegates' own forgiveness of the Japanese. He, in turn, asked for forgiveness for the sins of the Korean people, for their deep feelings of hatred toward the Japanese people. During the conference these Japanese and Korean delegates held late-night prayer meetings, confessing their sins to God and to one another, weeping. They then exchanged prayers and songs of blessings with one another. Finally they decided that this ministry of reconciliation that God had started must continue, so they formed the Japanese and Korean Student Fellowship. This incredible ministry of reconciliation is still continuing actively today.

In his prayer on the night before his crucifixion (John 17), Jesus prayed that his followers would become one so that the world would believe that he was sent by God. Genuine unity among Christians loudly proclaims the power and the truth of the good news of Jesus Christ. As our society becomes more fragmented and balkanized along race, gender and class lines, this mandate of witnessing through unity becomes particularly important to today's church. As the preceding story illustrates, genuine unity often calls for genuine reconciliation and repentance that honestly addresses past and present wrongdoings and pains.

The apostle Paul reminds us in Ephesians 2:11-22 that we can participate in the ministry of reconciliation because Jesus already has broken down dividing walls, the walls of hostility among different people groups. Jesus is not calling us to achieve a seemingly impossible dream. He is calling us to appropriate what he already has accomplished, to receive the grace of his forgiveness and to experience the grace of his healing power.

The tragic event of the Los Angeles riots was a turning point in my own journey of racial reconciliation and repentance. During that week I was beginning to read through the book of Isaiah. God confronted me about my unresolved attitudes of hostility toward African-American people and my lack of concern toward the poor and other marginalized people in our society. One morning in particular, as I humbly offered my prayer of repentance before God, I began to weep—for my sins, for the pains of fellow Korean Americans in Los Angeles, and for the pains of African-Americans and other oppressed people groups in our society! This was the beginning of a healing process for me. It was the beginning of a new journey in my growth as an agent of reconciliation.

Agents of Reconciliation: Peter

A few years ago, in the magazine *Christianity Today,* a number of African-American Christian leaders expressed their deep disappointment over the lack of progress made in the area of racial reconciliation within the church. Some even expressed a sense of deep hurt, feeling that they had been abandoned by their white brothers and sisters. (See Andrés Tapia, "The Myth of Racial Progress," October 4, 1993)

Thus far the ministry of racial reconciliation has been framed in the church as a black-white issue, partly because other race groups, including Asian Americans, have not actively participated in the process. But if the tragic event of the Los Angeles riots taught us anything, it is that Korean Americans and other Asian Americans no longer can see ourselves as casual spectators watching "race wars" from the sidelines.

Last fall I had just finished lecturing on the topic of racism in a course I was teaching at a seminary. Because the topic of racism and racial reconciliation had become an important issue for me, I spoke rather passionately. I think I preached to my class that day. After the class one of the students approached me and said, "You know, if you were a Caucasian professor and said what you said, African-Americans and other minority students might think, *He is speaking out of white guilt. Talk is cheap, you know; we need to see some action.* If you were an African-American professor and spoke on the topic with the same intensity, some of our Caucasian students might think, *Here we go again, another angry African-American person speaking out of black anger.* But with you being an Asian American person, we can't easily categorize you or label you. I think most of us heard your challenge on this issue in a fresh way."

This conversation with my student reminded me once again about the unique location Asian Americans occupy in the racial discourse in America. We do not carry with us the historical baggage of being former slave masters or former slaves. We are not yet labeled or categorized in a black-and-white way. This third-party position in which we find ourselves can offer us some unique opportunities to carry out the ministry of racial reconciliation.

I believe we Asian Americans can play this role with some effectiveness also because we occupy a unique place in the socio-economic structure in the U.S. On the one hand, as an ethnic minority group, Asian Americans continue to struggle with various forms of racism and prejudice. On the other hand, compared with other ethnic minority groups, Asian Americans as a group have more resources available to them. In short we are uniquely situated between the haves and the have-nots, between the powerful and the powerless in our society.

Because we, too, experience the hurts of being marginalized and powerless, we can offer our genuine compassion and empathy to our brothers and sisters who are less fortunate, serving them with humility and sensitivity. We can serve as what Henri Nouwen called "wounded healers."

Some Practical Suggestions: Susan

Here are some practical possibilities you might consider to begin your journey toward becoming a person of racial reconciliation.

☐ *Go on a short-term overseas or U.S. urban crosscultural mission.* Live with black, Latino or other community leaders who have much to teach you. InterVarsity has some great "Urban Projects" in many major cities across the United States and also sponsors "Global Projects" in many countries around the world.

☐ *Consider joining or visiting a church of a different ethnicity.* Go with an open attitude toward learning how to worship God in very different ways (and time schedules!).

☐ *Seek further biblical teaching on justice.* Ask Christian leaders and teachers of the Word what they think the kingdom of God should look like. Search the Scriptures yourself for clearer perspectives on God's desire for this area. Any work by John Perkins is a great start.

☐ *Pursue intentionally developing one deep friendship with someone from a different race or ethnicity.* As they become comfortable, ask them to teach you about their culture and try to see what is of the kingdom in it. Be real. Be honest. Have fun. Enjoy the delightful things God brings in differences. Be patient. Endure. Forgive.

☐ *Pray for God's work of racial reconciliation in this world, in this country and in the church.* It is the work of the enemy to bring alienation, mistrust and violence. Ultimately, though we can try our best to live out the vision of the kingdom that we see in the Scriptures, only God can change people's hearts and bring peace.

Lord God, we thank you for your heart of justice and unity. We know that forgiveness and reconciliation are at the heart of what you love.

We see that many are in the captivity of racism and alienation. Please raise up Asian American Christians who are willing to risk and labor for racial healing. Impress your vision for a multiethnic kingdom upon our hearts. Give us hope that all things can be reconciled through your Son.

9 Spiritual Growth

Greg Jao

WE YEARN FOR A DEEPER KNOWLEDGE OF GOD. WE CRAVE A RICHER experience of his presence, and we long for a greater assurance of his love. And these yearnings, cravings, and longings drive our spirituality—the practices through which we develop our relationship with him.

Our Asian American experience profoundly shapes our spirituality. Some portions of our bicultural heritage sharpen our understanding of biblical truths. Others distort it. Some enhance our discipleship, others corrupt it. Many of us, for example, come from faith communities that modeled the Confucian values of duty, community and altruistic self-sacrifice. Our churches, therefore, often reveal great faithfulness, deep sacrifice, committed prayer, obedience to Scripture, meaningful community, concern for family, and strong missions awareness. And our actions are powered by a keen sense of the holiness of God, the cost of Christ's death on the cross, and an awareness of our dependence on the Holy Spirit.

Many of us, however, recognize the partial cultural captivity of our spirituality. Burdened with a keen awareness of China's five thousand years of continuous history, for example, many Chinese Americans express a faith that is steady and pragmatic, but that generally avoids taking risks. In contrast, shaped by a shamanistic folk culture and Korean revival movements in the early 1900s, many Korean Americans demonstrate great faith, but often unreflectively insist that genuine worship and prayer is marked by volume, passion and catharsis. On the other hand, Japanese Americans, steeped in the culture of *wabi* (the unpretentious and harmonious expression of beauty) and *tsurasa* (a strong empathic response to another's pain), often think reflectively about faith but often fail to act boldly. We've seen that we have much to learn from each other. Chinese could grow in faithful expectancy, Koreans in quiet reflection, and Japanese in pragmatic boldness.

Common to almost all our spirituality, however, is a deep and often unverbalized sense of defeat, exhaustion, fear, and despair. We ache with the desire to be cherished by God, but our heavenly Father seems like just one more authority figure we are doomed to disappoint. We surreptitiously look for a smile of approval, the suggestion of an embrace, or an expression of delight. But we aren't surprised when we think we don't see it. Our cultural heritage shapes our experience and understanding of each member of the Trinity.

Father God—Distant, Detached, Demanding

It's appropriate that our relationship with our parents shapes our understanding of God. After all, God invites this comparison by revealing himself in Scripture as our Father. Not surprisingly, our cultural backgrounds mold our attitudes toward and our methods of approaching him.

For example, most of our family structures reflect the Confucian values of hierarchy, restraint and achievement. Confucius states, "Let the prince be a prince, the minister a minister, the father a father, and the son a son" (*Analects* 12.11). Our fathers, ruling the family from atop the hierarchy, occupy a social station that is both distinct from and superior to our own. As we consciously or unconsciously apply this understanding of fatherhood to God, our understanding of God's transcendence, sovereignty and holiness is sharpened. We recognize that our holy God reigns supreme from his heavenly throne. And our churches often have a strong tradition of reverence in worship, faith in prayer, and righteousness in lifestyle. But Asian American family dynamics also may distort our understanding of God. Many of us, for example, find it difficult to imagine significant intimacy between us and our parents. Hierarchy precludes egalitarian relationships, a key criterion of intimacy in a Western context. Not surprisingly, we don't feel intimate with God. He seems too holy to approach or to know.

In a recent prayer meeting, I was startled as a quiet woman next to me burst out in prayer: "God, we are not worthy to come to you! How can you stand us in your presence, O God? You are so holy and so good, but we are sinful, broken vessels. We do not understand why you accept our worship." Though I rejoiced over her sharp awareness of God's holiness, I grieved that she seemed unaware that God inhabits the worship of his people, delights as we approach him through Christ, and has revealed himself from Genesis through Revelation as a God who persistently seeks the lost.

What is our God like? In the parable of the searching father (what we often call the parable of the prodigal son), Jesus implies that the father faithfully searches the horizon for a trace of his lost child, until, one day, his straining eyes catch sight of the prodigal in the distance. The father doesn't hesitate. He doesn't wait for the child to come closer. The father does something amazing. He runs. He runs to the prodigal, embraces him and kisses this child who sinfully squandered everything. The lost has been found. Almost before the prodigal begins to mumble out an apology, he knows he is welcomed. Cherished. Embraced.

We worship a God who searches for us. Who runs. Who embraces us. And who celebrates as he welcomes us into his presence. Our God is both tremendously distant and shockingly close. This can be hard to believe.

A Cold God and a Hot Faith

Confucian restraint and deference also shape our spirituality. Many Asian parents (fathers especially) model emotional and verbal restraint. Though we may converse with them, we may not converse deeply. The topics skitter from school to work to family, like a rock sent skipping along the shore. We often expect that our parents will disclose little of what they are thinking and feeling. And we expect as little from God.

Many of us respond to silence with either polite formality or unrelieved chatter. In some Chinese church circles, for example, prayer becomes an exercise in *ke qi*, the demonstration of proper deference and respect. We offer fervent prayers, but mostly because propriety demands it, not necessarily because we recognize that God is present. This approach to prayer resembles the lip service paid at a plurality of religious altars by millions throughout Chinese Asia. Planting incense sticks at Buddhist, Taoist and animist shrines, many Chinese fervently—but mechanically—attempt to purchase "insurance" from all religions in the off-chance that one of them is correct.

By contrast, in some Korean church circles, we experience an unrelenting torrent of prayer. Prayer becomes an unstoppable human monologue in which the person pleads with God to forgive, begs that God act and beseeches God to reveal himself. Our prayers often resemble shamans prying favors from the capricious spirit world, rather than worshipers of a gracious, generous God.

And what applies to prayer applies to our Bible study, worship and the other spiritual disciplines. We don't expect a meaningful conversation with God, just as we don't expect a meaningful conversation with our parents. But the parable of the searching father reminds us that the father desires to respond. The petulant elder child demands, "Why do you celebrate for him? Why waste even more on that prodigal?" And perhaps more quietly, more fearfully, "Would you have done the same for *me?*"

The father answers. He speaks to the embittered son who, in that moment, is as lost as the prodigal ever was. He answers all of the child's fearsome and fearful questions. And he loves him. "Son," he says, "you are always with me, and all that is mine is yours" (Luke 15:31).

Our God desires to speak, as well as to listen; to initiate, as well as to respond; to give good gifts, as well as to receive worship. God offers us a meaningful relationship—partnership, interaction and conversation—rather than reserved silence. But we often don't listen.

Is There Good News in the Gospel?

We may believe God accepts us, but we're convinced he settled for damaged goods. We can't understand why God chose us. We acknowledge that he forgives our sins, but we cannot comprehend his joyful acceptance of sinful people. Beyond proper feelings of guilt (moral culpability), we struggle with an intense sense of shame (inherent unacceptability).

Coming from group-oriented cultures, we construct our identity through community-defined expectations. Therefore, a failure to satisfy these community-defined obligations defines our identity. We experience shame. When we fail to satisfy others' expectations, we internalize the message *Not only have I failed, but I am a failure.* Studies confirm that Asian Americans experience disproportionately strong feelings of shame compared with others. And we experience shame primarily in terms of feeling deficient and exposed (Warden, "Issues of Internalized Shame in Asian-Americans").

Shame often arises when we fail to meet our parents' expectations. Not only have we failed to achieve, but we have failed to be the children that our parents want us to be. Similarly, when we sin we not only have violated God's commands, but also have failed to be the disciples that God wants us to be. Our feelings may be objectively correct (we may not be the children or disciples that our parents and our God desire for us to be), but the intensity of our experience of shame is disproportionately crippling. Our inability to satisfy our parents' lofty goals and our God's seemingly impossible standards has etched the experience of shame doubly deeply into our souls. And our experience of shame often causes us to miss the heart of the gospel.

Empty cornfields rolled by as a colleague described his prayer experiences at a recent student convention. "I prayed for one Asian American student who was really agitated," he told me. "Even though the conference focused on God's extravagant and unconditional love for the world, all this student said he had heard was 'a message of condemnation.' The student prayed: 'You are so good to me, and you are so merciful. You have blessed me in so many ways. But I am so unworthy. I try and try, but I fail all the time. I am not worthy to be your son, Father God. How can you love me?' There seemed to be little good news in the gospel for that student."

As I passed a slow-moving car, my friend remarked: "It was really sad. This guy had no concept of grace, no assurance of forgiveness and no idea about the cross. All he knew was that God wanted more from him and he couldn't cut it. I really felt like God was telling me just to pray truth to him—truth about God's love, about the cross and about who he was in Christ."

A Christless Christianity

Perhaps it is easier for most of us to focus on the first person of the Trinity, God the Father. Asian cultures are both patriarchal and hierarchical. Furthermore, many Asian Americans sharply feel the emotional deficits associated with our apparently distant and emotionally detached fathers. Therefore, we focus on God as Father more easily. And as an unintentional result, Jesus and his work on the cross are deemphasized. At best we see Jesus as the example of the horrific cost the Father paid to redeem humanity. At worst Jesus fuels our shame when we consider our inability to obey God in light of Christ's obedient suffering.

A colleague once related his experience with an Asian American student at an evangelistic training session. He found her technique telling. "I basically tell them that God is our Father and that he loves us," she explained. "He gives us many good things so we should believe in him. And that's about it," she concluded brightly.

Tentatively, my colleague asked, "What about Christ and the cross—or sin?"

"Oh, I don't understand any of that stuff," she replied, "so I don't talk about it too much."

We are poorer without a meaningful understanding of the cross. Without the cross we have no assurance that we are forgiven and accepted by the Father.

Scholar Kenneth Bailey has pointed out that the parable of the searching father would have shocked Middle Eastern peasants for the same reason the cross shocks us today. The whole village would have expected the father to preserve his honor by inflicting punishment after the lost child approached, groveled and blurted out an apology. Instead, this father runs. Elderly men in the Middle East never run, but this father runs down the street to meet his son. In so running, the searching father "takes upon himself the shame and the humiliation due the prodigal" (Bailey, *Through Peasant Eyes*).

It is Christ who most clearly reveals the character of the Father. In Christ's horrific death on the cross, our God took upon himself all of our sin and all of our shame. On the cross he became shameful so that we could be shameless. The bloody cross insists that we are guilty sinners who should feel shame. But the bloody cross also reminds us that nothing—neither our sin nor our shame—can separate us from the extravagant love of God. We need a faith based on the cross.

Saving Face and Losing Grace

For the student who was helped by my colleague at the conference, hearing the truth about Christ in the context of the community of Christ brought healing. But often shame hinders our ability to enjoy true Christian community. It forbids us from acknowledging the sin and struggle in our lives. Asking for help requires an admission that everything is not all right, causing us to lose face. Therefore, we save face and lose the opportunity to experience the grace of Christ mediated through the people of Christ. We try to look and act like real followers of Jesus, and in so doing, we demonstrate that we do not know Jesus at all.

Ironically, identifying ourselves as followers of Jesus should free us from the need to save face. As Christians, we already have acknowledged publicly that we are defeated by sin. In fact, we gather together in churches precisely because we are sinners. We have no face to lose, but we live as if we do.

When we choose to live without a concern for face, however, we free the people of Christ to act as the body of Christ. A pastor friend often tells of his experience in an Asian American men's discipleship group. As they met, my friend made the decision to speak transparently and vulnerably about his own battle with temptation. "Once I began to share openly," he explains, "the rest of the group was free to share honestly as well. We gained the opportunity to pray truthfully for each other, hold each other accountable and encourage each other. We had nothing to hide. And we got a tremendous sense of what it means to live in true community."

Prodigals should always return to celebration and welcome. When the prodigal in the parable returns home, the searching father welcomes him back publicly. (The village would have gathered when the calf was slaughtered.) The father releases the son from shame by initiating him back into the community. It's clear from the elder child's comments that the prodigal's sinfulness is known. But there is no cover-up, because it's equally clear that the father has forgiven. So the community celebrates.

Communities of Shame

Unfortunately, those of us who choose to save face often find ourselves attracted to spiritually abusive communities. Our intense sense of shame blocks our ability to recognize the saving effect of Christ's death. As a result, we seek spiritual leaders and groups who focus almost exclusively on convicting us of sin, pointing out our lack of passion and demanding legalistic conformity. Though all Christians must acknowledge sin, abusive ministries focus on sin to the exclusion of forgiveness and restoration.

Spiritually abusive leaders and groups attract shame-filled people for three reasons. First, the repeated condemnations reinforce our self-diagnosis and confirm our worst fears: we are not worthy to be close to God. Perversely, this confirmation masochistically pleases us. It validates our self-assessment: *I was right! I'm not worthy.*

Second, many of us equate guilt feelings with divine conviction. Abusive ministries create the guilty feelings that we associate with the Holy Spirit's activity. One Canadian teacher with a large ministry boasts that he has "the gift of rebuking." Unfortunately, the regular cycle of intense guilt inducement creates an addictive pattern of emotional and spiritual bulimia. We binge and purge our shame.

Third, we believe we deserve abusive situations. Ken Blue notes in *Healing Spiritual Abuse*, "A severe sense of guilt prompts us to hate what we have done. This pain may drive us to repent and make restitution. A severe sense of shame, on the other hand, prompts us to hate who we are. . . . Shame calls for punishment, which is exactly what abusive leaders offer."

Eventually, spiritually abusive conditions become the norm by which we judge other Christians. One individual told his pastor, "I cannot worship with you because you aren't Asian enough—you don't rebuke us enough. You don't call us to commitment. I don't think that you take faith seriously." Another individual told me, "Your church group talks too much about grace."

As if the church *could* talk too much about grace.

Taking Works Seriously

Our spirituality emerges not only from shame-based cultures but also from cultures that are steeped in Confucian performance orientation and that have discovered that hard work can provide economic security. Coupled with the Western "can-do" spirit, Asian Americans often demonstrate a powerful work ethic bordering on workaholism. Therefore, it is not surprising that many of us turn to the Asian American work ethic for an appropriate spirituality.

Positively, Asian American faith often is expressed in giving, participating and serving. We give our time to Bible studies, prayer meetings, revival meetings and church services. We offer our money. And we provide our services to youth activities, church conferences and congregational leadership. Even when Asian Americans constituted a small minority of the students within InterVarsity, a disproportionate number rose to leadership positions. And as our numbers increased, multiethnic fellowships often needed to work intentionally to ensure that non-Asians became involved in worship and organizational leadership. God seems to bless our ministries.

Our performance orientation can betray us, however. Our works-oriented, production-driven faith often leads us into pride. Our attitudes imply that we see results in ministry and in life because of the fervency of our prayers, the faithfulness of our service or the generosity of our giving. We attribute our relative financial success to our positive attitudes, unflinching work ethic and Confucian paradigms. But we often fail to acknowledge that our success comes from the gracious hand of God. We lack thankfulness and humility. We rob God of the glory due him. And we refuse to recognize his grace.

When we refuse to accept grace from God, we often also refuse to receive grace—unmerited acceptance, forgiveness, encouragement and accountability—from others. Acknowledging need terrifies us because it forces us to lose face by admitting weakness. It demands that we impose on others to supply our lack. It reminds us that our individual activity may not be enough to save us.

Worst of all, our performance orientation prevents us from extending grace to others. Like us, the elder child in the parable of the searching father listened well to the cultural influences that encouraged performance and achievement. He worked faithfully. He served quietly. And he complained bitterly as his father offered grace to his younger brother. He revealed himself to be a prodigal as well.

A Faithless Faith

A performance spirituality can cause us to believe that our passion and commitment reflect the quality of our relationship with God. Carol, an InterVarsity staff worker, once said to me, "The Asian American students in my chapter are often the hardest working students. They'll come to every retreat, every prayer meeting and every large group meeting whether they feel like it or not. Sometimes their dedication is a relief in comparison to my Anglo students, who only show up when they want to." She paused. "At other times, though, the best thing I can do for them is to tell them not to come. They're shocked when I do it, but they start to confuse faith with faithful attendance."

Our beliefs about grace may be orthodox, but we have not appropriated the truth that we are saved by grace alone. Our lifestyles demonstrate that we really believe that the more we do, the more we will be loved. And when we cannot do more, we cannot be loved. And so we do more. We go to more meetings, pray more passionately, worship more fervently, give more generously and serve more sacrificially. And slowly we become trapped in a never-ending treadmill of obligations, requirements and meetings. We find God and God's work exhausting. We develop a faith from which the cross of Christ is missing.

One summer I was visiting Ben, an Asian American student who was in the hospital for minor surgery. To encourage him, I shared my appreciation for his evangelistic gifts. He had meaningfully and faithfully shared his faith and life with dozens of people that year. Ben's response shocked me. "But I'm not faithful, Greg," he said with real despair. "I try hard to be obedient, to do the right thing. But I keep failing. I keep sinning. How can God love me? People who love God don't keep sinning. How can I be a Christian when I am such a sinner?"

I thought about the parable of the searching father before I answered. In the story the father cherishes both the profligate and the dutiful, the repentant and the embittered, the joyful and the joyless. His actions are unmerited and unrequired. He leaves his home and goes out to both of his prodigal children. He invites them to celebrate and vividly reminds both of them that he is their father. He offers grace.

"How can you be anything *but* a Christian if you are such a sinner?" I asked in reply. "Have you forgotten about the cross? Have you forgotten that the apostle Paul called himself the chief of sinners?" I leaned over the bed rail and looked him in the eyes. "Christ died in vain if we could be perfect on our own. He died to forgive all our sin—past, present and future. Ben, you don't have to be good to be acceptable to God. You have to be forgiven."

A New Freedom, an Unstable Passion

If our Asian American heritage causes us to overemphasize God's distance and underemphasize the work of Jesus on the cross, it also causes us to misunderstand the Holy Spirit. Driven, perhaps, by our experience with emotionally inexpressive parents and our discomfort with Asian emotional restraint, we often seek the experience of freedom and boldness brought by the Holy Spirit. As a result, we've developed a greater ability to express our hearts. We often have become communities marked by passion and joy.

Unfortunately, some of us are known better for our boldness than for our thoughtfulness. Though we worship passionately, we do not worship well, because we know little about the God whom we worship. Our commitment to Bible study, Christian thinking and meaningful theological reflection often fails to match our commitment to catharsis. As a result, our words, deeds and expectations can demonstrate great breadth without significant depth. We forget that the Spirit not only desires to bring greater boldness, creativity and freedom but also offers wisdom, discernment and order.

A friend leading a missions project to a closed country expressed dismay at the negative impact created by a group of Asian missionaries prior to his arrival. "They came with a lot of money and big plans and made a lot of noise," he said. "They tried to organize a March for Jesus in the middle of the capital. As a result, they got kicked out of the country, all pending visas were canceled—including ours—and the government focused a lot of negative attention on the local church."

"What were they thinking?" I asked.

"They weren't. They wanted to make a 'bold statement for Jesus.' All they really accomplished was to make a big excuse for persecution." Wise boldness is a mark of the Holy Spirit.

We also can detrimentally equate emotional experience and passion with the Holy Spirit's activity. We forget that the Holy Spirit is a person, not an experience. We can confuse our subjective experiences of worship, confession and action with our relationship with God. Our subjective approach to faith leaves us unable and unwilling to walk obediently and faithfully through difficult or painful times. Dry or dark periods become synonymous with a loss of faith rather than a seasonal experience of the soul. We have no discipline in our spiritual disciplines. We have no endurance. And so we have no hope.

I remember sitting in a Thai restaurant near the University of Chicago with a student. "I'm having a hard time keeping my faith," he admitted over dinner. "In high school I felt very close to God. I could feel him with me. Now I don't feel anything at all. I wonder if he was really ever there." The obvious fruit of the Spirit in his life, the witness of Scripture and the testimony of his friends were insufficient to convince him that God was there. Without immediate, palpable experience, his faith collapsed.

Our spirituality needs to be grounded not only in internal experience but also in the external record of other people who have witnessed the outworking of God's character and attributes. The young prodigal of the parable of the searching father knows this truth well. Lusting after scraps and sleeping with swine, he begins his journey home only when he recalls witnessing the generosity of his father to the family servants. At that moment he knows his father better than he ever has. And it is enough. He returns home. And he is welcomed.

We need to make ourselves familiar with God's character by systematically studying the whole of Scripture, not just our favorite texts; by engaging in the sustained conversation of prayer, listening as well as speaking; and by enfolding our intercession in an expectant envelope of recognition and recollection of God's character.

Finding the True Counselor

Driven by our own sense of distance from God, many of us are attracted to experiences of deep community and to authority figures with genuine spiritual sensitivity to mediate our relationship with God. To a certain degree, this attraction arises from the high value placed on community and the honor given to people with special access to the spirit world—monks, bodhisattvas, shamans and priests—in Asian cultures. Positively, this tendency helps us value the body of Christ and develop a generally strong respect for the pastorate. These tendencies also fuel a desire among many unchurched Asian Americans to enter into Christian fellowship.

Negatively, however, as a group-oriented people we can confuse the experience of community with an experience of Christ. We can offer commitment to the people of Christ rather than wholehearted obedience to the person of Christ. And we can experience our community's failures as Christ's failures.

We also can unquestioningly seek and blindly accept prophecies or words of wisdom from leaders who equate obedience to God with submission to their statements. Preying on our perceived distance from God and our deference to the spiritually powerful, they dictatorially direct our vocational, spousal and spiritual choices. In response we abdicate our responsibility to discern from Scripture, in community, and through prayer whether they truly speak words from God and of God.

But if we unreflectively accept the words of these leaders, we despise the Spirit's work in our lives. We deny that the Holy Spirit indwells each of us—granting discernment, illumining Scripture, and providing insight and guidance. Leaders genuinely gifted and properly motivated by the Holy Spirit will honor the Spirit by encouraging us to seek confirmation of their words. After all, it is the same Spirit that inspired Scripture, moves in our fellowship and guides our prayers. But we doubt our ability to discern rightly and to hear God correctly. We struggle with our sense of spiritual deficiency.

Gifts to All for All

We struggle even with the belief that we have been meaningfully gifted by the Spirit. Intensely aware of our unworthiness, trained to avoid self-assertion and self-promotion, and encouraged to be self-deprecating, we hesitate to affirm that we have gifts of value to the church and the world. The Holy Spirit, though, is lavish and impartial in his distribution of gifts. He gives gifts to all. When we deny our gifting, we implicitly reject the Holy Spirit's gifts and dispute his generosity.

If we recognize our gifting, our Confucian and Western backgrounds often cause us to value public gifts—including teaching, prophesying, leading and pastoring—more highly than behind-the-scenes gifts—including serving, helping, encouraging and studying. We are acutely sensitive to the strong, though unhealthy, distinction between the ordained ministry and laity in most of our immigrant churches. We assume that the blessing or petition of a pastor is more effective. But if we value others' gifts more highly than our own, we are ungrateful recipients of the Spirit's gifts. We cannot jealously eye the gifts of another and simultaneously give thanks for the gifts we have received. All of our gifts are necessary. As we work in community, the diversity of our gifts works symbiotically to serve the church in its work of glorifying God in the world.

It is in community and in glorifying God in the world that our gifts are best identified. As we serve and take steps of faith, we begin to identify the gifts the Spirit has given us—whether natural or supernatural—in a more definitive way than taking a spiritual gifts inventory. And as we serve, we allow the body of Christ to affirm that the Holy Spirit has gifted us all to serve all.

True spirituality must be expressed and discovered in community. Even though this chapter has examined the way our Asian cultures nurture and twist our spirituality, it displays a distinctly individualistic Western bias: it focuses exclusively on the private spiritual life of the believer. Genuine biblical spirituality is practiced in community, a truth our group-oriented Asian cultures value highly. And genuine spirituality will push us to serve others—Christian and not-yet-Christian, Asian and non-Asian, male and female, poor and rich—a truth our profoundly individualistic Western and generally xenophobic Asian backgrounds tend to obscure.

Our relationship with God cannot be experienced merely in worship, prayer or Bible study. It must also be expressed as evangelism, through social action and in predetermined acts of kindness. As we begin to speak and to live out the spiritual, political, economic and social implications of the good news, we will begin to know the heart of God. Other chapters in this book have sketched out how God desires us to restore wholeness and righteousness to family, gender and racial relationships. But God desires to transform the practices and systems of our workplaces, neighborhoods and countries as well, another truth our privatized Western and ethnocentric Asian cultures can obscure. We must offer all of our gifts—both personal and cultural—to the world.

The Searching God

We seek a God who persistently searches for us.

He craves a richer experience of our presence, and he longs for the trusting acceptance of his love. We may believe that God turns his face as we stagger toward him, reeking of sin and encrusted by shame. But he sees us. We may fear that he wouldn't even notice if we were missing from the party as we remain outside, defeated by frustration, despair and depression. But he sees us, the profligate and the prideful, the licentious and the legalistic, the broken and the bitter. He sees us. And he runs—toward us.

My child has come home.

His embrace awaits us. He knows us. He welcomes us. He cherishes us. And he celebrates.

The lost has been found.

He is a searching father indeed.

10 Finding a Church Home

Peter Cha

"SO YOU ARE NOT COMING BACK TO OUR CHURCH?" ASKED MY FATHER.
I was about to graduate from seminary, and I was on the phone to tell
my father that I had decided not to return to my Korean American home
church. After a long pause, he asked, "Don't you think the Korean
American church desperately needs an English-speaking person like
you?"

I don't quite remember how the rest of the conversation went. What
I do still remember is how I felt after I hung up the phone. I felt like I
really let down my father and the people in my home church who
nurtured me.

For many Asian Americans the quest to find the right church can be
complicated and even messy. For one thing, for many of us this task
becomes more than just a spiritual project. When we choose to return
to our ethnic home churches or to belong to "other" churches, whether
we intend it or not, we also communicate how we relate to our own
ethnic identities and to our cultures and communities. For those of us
whose journeys of faith and of ethnic identity formation are intertwined, finding the right church involves more than looking into the
church's worship style.

And then, for some of us, the task of looking for a healthy church is itself problematic because we feel that the phrase "healthy church" is an oxymoron. Unfortunately, many of us grew up in Asian immigrant churches where we experienced much pain, frustration and disappointment. We can depend on and love our God, and many of us have really enjoyed our college Christian fellowship experiences. Some of us, however, are not quite sure if we can trust "church," let alone be a part of it. "I am a Christian, but I don't have to be a church-going Christian," some of us declare, and then elect to be lone-ranger Christians.

Distorted Images of Church

In *Sometimes It's Hard to Love God,* a Christian psychologist points out how our past, unhealthy relationships with our parents can distort our images of the heavenly Father, thus making it difficult for us to experience a loving and healthy relationship with him. Similarly, for many of us, our past church experiences continue to warp our understanding of what church is, thus hindering our healthy participation in it. A study shows that well over 75 percent of American-born Chinese in Chinese immigrant churches end up leaving their churches (Joseph Wong, "Bridging the Gap," *About Face*). Some informal studies indicate that up to 90 percent of postcollege Korean American young people are also leaving their immigrant churches. In an attempt to make sense of our immigrant church experiences, many of us constructed certain images of our churches based on our own experiences and views.

☐ *Art museum.* Some of us perceived our churches to be a place where people incessantly talked about achievements of their own or of their children. For many young people the church was gradually identified as a place where people come together to show off, even if it is done in a very self-effacing Asian way.

☐ *Ethnic cultural center.* "If you lose the tongue, you lose the faith" was the unspoken axiom in some of our churches. Interracial dating and marriage was frowned upon, if not strongly discouraged. Subtle or not-so-subtle messages of ethnocentricism were taught. Our church was for our kind of people only.

☐ *Pseudo-extended family.* Some of us perceived our churches to be a place where tight relationships were formed around loyalty, responsibility and hierarchy. Often there was a strong pastor or other leadership figures who acted as our surrogate parents and older siblings.

An Exercise of Remembrance
Given the preceding images of the church, it's no wonder that so many of our friends have left our churches and that so many of us are not excited about the idea of becoming an active member of a church. For many of us, therefore, the first step we need to take as we think about our future church involvement—whether we are planning to return to our ethnic immigrant churches or are thinking of joining other churches—is to be engaged prayerfully in a process of remembering our past immigrant church experiences.

The first part of this process of remembrance should be thanksgiving—giving thanks to God for the many blessings we have received through our immigrant church experiences. My experiences in Korean immigrant churches have been both positive and negative. As a person who grew up in Korean immigrant churches and later served in these churches as a pastoral staff member, it is easy for me to be very critical of Korean immigrant churches. And when I am in such a mindset, I so easily forget the many blessings God has given me through these congregations. Recently, while visiting the Los Angeles area where I spent my early adolescent years, I met with a number of old church friends and reminisced about our youth group experiences. In the midst of our remembrance and laughter, it dawned on me once again how much of who I am today is due to what I received and experienced through that small Korean immigrant congregation in Los Angeles.

I am grateful that I served and grew under many godly Korean American pastors, including my father, who loved the Lord and sacrificially served the church. I am also thankful that my church tradition has drilled into me the importance of prayer and sacrificial giving to God's work, two of many spiritual attributes that characterize the Korean Christian heritage. I know that much of who I am as a Christian has been shaped by my family and church upbringing. What blessings have you received through your immigrant church ministry?

At the same time, this exercise of remembrance also calls us to forgive our churches for the ways that they have hurt us. An Asian American woman once told me how she and her family were ostracized in a Korean immigrant church because she was being brought up by a divorced mother (the family was abandoned by the father). She remembered with much pain that many parents in her church actively discouraged their children from playing with her and her siblings. She and her family were victims of our strong cultural prejudice against those who are socially different, those who do not fit into certain norms. The deeply tragic aspect of her experience was that it happened in the church, the place where mercy and love should abound. Perhaps some of us have similar stories to tell. If we are to receive healing from these painful memories, however, we need to take the step of forgiving our churches . . . and move on.

A Divine and Human Reality

Another step toward having a healthy relationship with the church involves our recognition of the paradoxical truth that the church is both divine and human. On the one hand, the Scriptures teach us that the church is a glorious, spiritual entity. This means that, recognizing its divine reality, we should not look at any church with disdain, including those immigrant churches that may have disappointed us deeply or even harmed us. For no matter how imperfect it might be, the church is nonetheless the body of Christ, a precious gift from our God.

At the same time, the church is a human institution. Growing up as a "PK" (pastor's kid), I saw the human side of the church all too vividly—continuous gossip, power struggles, church fights and splits. By the time I was going off to college, I was ready to say "goodby" to church, and I did for a while. A part of my maturing process as a Christian involved the recognition that church is also a human institution, that it is a community made up of sinners who so desperately need God's healing touch and his redeeming grace in their lives.

Our understanding of this dual nature of church is critical in shaping a healthy, balanced and biblical view of church. It reminds us that we should avoid the error of idealizing our church, expecting our church to be perfect. A pastor on the radio once challenged his listeners, "If you were never happy at any church and you are constantly looking for the perfect church, let me give you advice. If you happen to find a perfect church, don't join it, because you will ruin it." Those of us who had negative experiences in our immigrant churches particularly can easily think that our church-related problems and struggles will end if we turn to other, "nonimmigrant" churches. Guess what? Different churches have different sets of challenges and struggles—there are no perfect churches.

Furthermore, our recognition that church is both divine and human helps us to better understand and appreciate the unique nature and challenge of our immigrant churches. From the beginning immigrant churches have played multiple roles in our communities. They could not simply function as spiritual communities when there were so many varied and urgent needs in our immigrant families and communities. The fact that our churches play these multiple, sociocultural roles is not bad or unbiblical. In fact, because they played these sociocultural roles so effectively, many of our parents and their peers have become Christians.

What becomes problematic is when the immigrant church's various sociocultural roles become more visible and prominent than its spiritual functions as a church, or, to put it differently, when its own ethnic, traditional values and norms—rather than biblical values—shape the life of the church. My father, who served nearly twenty years as an immigrant church pastor, once summarized the main challenge of an immigrant church by using this imagery: "A boat needs water to travel on. But it would be disastrous if the water came in."

Considering a Homecoming?

Since the beginning of my seminary years, I have served in Korean immigrant churches ten years. During those years I always appreciated postcollege young people returning to their "home" churches to serve, particularly to mentor and teach their younger brothers and sisters in the church. In some ways their ministry was even more effective than mine. After all, I was a pastor; I was trained (and paid) to teach and to serve. These returning young adults, on the other hand, were volunteers in the purest sense of the word: they were there simply because they cared for and loved these students. Also, some of my youth group students saw how much some of these young adults had grown in Christ during their college years. They were a living testimony to the transforming power of the gospel.

After working three years as an engineer in another city, my younger brother James decided to come home to help my aging parents . . . and to help our home church with its growing youth ministry. During his college years he matured spiritually through the Navigators ministry, benefiting from its fine training programs as well as from its multiethnic community life. During those years, perhaps more than anything else, he learned that the kingdom of God is bigger than the Korean American Presbyterian Church. When he returned to our home church in the mid-eighties, he particularly challenged his students to catch the broader kingdom vision. He regularly took the students into Washington, D.C., to share the good news with non-Korean Americans and to care for the poor and the homeless in the city. Today some of the students from his early years of ministry are postcollege young adults, and many of them point out how James had stretched their ministry vision and brought renewal into this particular immigrant church's second-generation ministry. Is the Lord calling you to be such a catalyst, an agent of transformation in our immigrant churches?

Going home, or returning to our immigrant churches, however, may not be an easy option for some of us. This may be particularly true for women. Lisa was a president of a large InterVarsity chapter, a sister with proven leadership and a great heart for God and for the ministry of the gospel. She would have been a strong asset to any ministry, and she wanted to continue to serve God with the gifts he had given her. And yet, as she was thinking about life after graduation, she struggled greatly with the idea of returning to her home church. As much as she cared for her church, she also knew that she would not be able to freely exercise her gifts and talents in her church because she was a woman. She had to count the cost.

Another cost involved in returning to an immigrant church might be the fact that your immigrant church may not have a well-established English-speaking ministry for postcollege young adults. Often our immigrant churches lack spiritual mentors who speak English and who understand our struggles; often we are the oldest and wisest(?) among the English-speaking members, even though we may be just out of college! In many cases our church's English-speaking ministry is still geared toward the youth group crowd, not toward helping us directly with our postcollege discipleship. So, while serving younger brothers and sisters in the congregation, how do we continue to grow as followers of Jesus Christ? How do we avoid that inevitable burnout when we are constantly giving without receiving much?

While I was serving in my immigrant church, I regularly met with spiritual mentors and prayer partners who were not from my church. These spiritual uncles and aunts and brothers and sisters provided me with much-needed counsel and encouragement. They became the resource persons I could not find in my own church. Another wonderful benefit of having "outside" mentors was that I was constantly reminded of the reality of God's greater family outside of my own ethnic church. My mentor/prayer partners came from diverse ethnic and denominational backgrounds, constantly stretching me to grow in my understanding of and appreciation for the diverse nature of God's family. For those of us who find a home in ethnic immigrant churches, finding meaningful mentoring and fellowship activities outside our own churches is a must. Are there people you can approach for such relationships? Will you prayerfully initiate (in most cases I had to) these relationships?

Finally, another word of advice for those of us who are returning to our immigrant churches. Perhaps some of us are excited about homecoming because we have much to share and to give. We have experienced wonderful growth and received much training through our campus ministry experiences, and we can't wait until we bring some change to our home church. Before jumping in with a million new ideas and tons of good intentions, it would be wise to think about the central ministry value our Lord Jesus demonstrated for us: servanthood. Especially during the initial time of ministry, would we be willing to serve the church humbly and patiently? Are we willing to serve with those who might not share our vision or agree with our new ideas? I have seen many postcollege young people return to their home churches with many ministry ideas and tools; however, those who made lasting contributions to the life of the church were those who understood and practiced servanthood in their ministries.

Exploring Non-Asian Churches

When my wife, Phyllis, and I got married and moved to Indiana, we attended a Caucasian church for three years. Coming from a somewhat sheltered immigrant church experience, I had much to learn about the European American church culture and about how to serve in such a context. At first I was overwhelmed in the new setting. I was reluctant to become involved; I tried to rationalize that because the church offered such a fine preaching/teaching ministry, simply coming to Sunday-morning worship services would be sufficient for Phyllis's and my spiritual growth. But I am glad that God prompted us to do more than that. During those years we actively participated in the church ministry as teachers of an adult Sunday-school class and as small group leaders.

Through those experiences I have learned that not only do I have a lot to learn from my European American brothers and sisters, but that I also have a lot to offer them. As I became more actively involved in church life, I learned that I can enjoy very intimate relationships with my Hoosier European American brothers and sisters simply because we are one in Christ. Indeed, our small group experience in that church, meeting with five other newlywed couples for three years, has been one of the richest fellowship experiences we have had . . . and these friends didn't even know what kimchee was.

There was another surprising benefit. It was in this new setting, ironically, that God began to deepen my understanding of and appreciation for my own Korean spiritual heritage. The famous poet J. W. von Goethe once said that one who does not know another language does not fully know one's own. During my years in that non-Asian church, I was able to reflect on both the strengths and weaknesses of my Korean spiritual heritage—I began to learn how to critique and affirm what I had inherited from my parents.

Finally, another wonderful benefit of belonging to such a church was that we were able to find many wise mentors in the church. Dr. Charles Smith was one of our mentors; he taught us many lessons about financial stewardship and our participation in world missions. It's been ten years since we left that church in Indiana, but we still try to meet once a year for fellowship and ongoing mentoring. I thank God for these saints and for our positive experiences in non-Asian churches (our family recently belonged to another wonderful European American congregation for three years). Given my positive experiences in these churches, when Asian American students inquire about the possibility of being a part of a non-Asian church, I readily encourage them to prayerfully explore the possibility.

At the same time, there are some potential challenges and drawbacks in attending non-Asian churches. As mentioned earlier, when we attend a non-Asian church, the temptation is even greater to be a spectator, just to attend Sunday worship services. We feel we don't quite fit in because everything seems new and different. So we see ourselves as guests (and sometimes we are treated as guests). But to belong to a church means to be an active, participating member, not only receiving but also giving, not only responding but also initiating. You may have found a church that offers excellent ministries, but if you don't intentionally get involved, are you receiving all that God is wanting you to receive? As an Asian American Christian, you also have something to offer to your new congregation. Take initiative! Get involved!

Another challenge is the possibility of not being affirmed about our ethnic identity in such a setting. God did not make a mistake when he brought me into this world through a Korean family and nurtured me through the Korean church and community. Therefore, for me, my faith development and my ethnic identity formation were intertwined processes that could not be separated easily. Thus, when our family decided to belong to a non-Asian church four years ago, one of the things we looked for was the church's appreciation of cultural diversity.

Looking for an Asian American Church?

Another church option for some of us is to belong to one of a growing number of churches that are intentionally serving and reaching out to English-speaking Asian Americans. In response to the growing number of Asian American young people leaving their immigrant churches and to the astonishing fact that up to 97 percent of Asian Americans are unchurched (according to a report by Stanley Inoye in the newsletter of an Asian American ministry consultant group called Iwa). Asian American churches are being formed in many metropolitan areas. Usually these churches are multiethnic. The church of which my family and I are currently a part (a year-old Asian American church) is a good example. Our congregation consists of Asian Americans who come from at least seven different Asian ethnic groups, plus a growing number of non-Asian American friends.

Those of us who are involved in an Asian American church appreciate a church's ministry that is informed and guided by the unique Asian American context. The goal of our church is to offer an outreach and discipleship ministry that will bring the truth revealed in the Word of God (the text) to our particular experiences and challenges (the context). For example, as Asian American Christians, how are we to practice God's commandment for us to honor our parents? Are we to blindly obey our parents, as our Confucian-based culture seems to teach? Or are we to learn to "hate" our parents for Christ's sake, as our non-Asian Christian friends frequently remind us? (Often non-Asian Christian friends use Luke 14:26 to emphasize that our discipleship may call for a decisive action of disobeying or even "hating" our parents.) Asian American churches provide a setting where we can come together and struggle with this question. We may not always come up with clear and satisfying answers to this and other challenging questions, but we can always count on support and encouragement from others who empathize with our deep struggles and pains.

Although most people in the church I am currently serving come from an Asian background, there are many different cultural and church traditions represented in our congregation. Diversity and differences always bring growing pains. During the past couple of years, for example, some of us noticed that Korean American brothers and sisters (including me) make decisions more intuitively (or, some might say, impulsively), whereas Chinese American brothers and sisters make their decisions more methodically. In working together, therefore, some of us had to learn how to be more reflective, while others had to learn how to take more risks in faith. Our diversity has stretched us as individuals and enriched us as a collective body, and we celebrate that.

Also, our life together is a testimony to God's healing work going on in the Asian American Christian community. We often wonder if a multiethnic Asian congregation would have been possible in our parents' generation. Given the deep historical animosities that existed among Asian countries, particularly between Japan and the rest of the Asian nations, it is very difficult to imagine Japanese Americans and other Asian Americans coming together as a church, learning to love and serve one another. Yes, we do all look alike, but behind our shared physical features are centuries-old hostilities and hatred that have effectively divided our peoples. One of the callings of Asian American churches is to be engaged intentionally in the ministry of reconciliation among our peoples.

While these Asian American churches might be multiethnic to a degree, most of them are not multiracial. An Asian American church might be more inclusive than a typical immigrant church, but it is nonetheless more focused in its mission and in identifying its target audience. Therefore, if you feel strongly about belonging to a church that ministers to a wider circle of people, an Asian American church may not be the best place for you.

Belonging to a Church

A well-known Christian counselor once said that a good marriage has more to do with *being* the right person than with *finding* the right person. Likewise, I wonder if our relationship with a local church also requires a similar commitment. Finding the right church is an important, if not elusive, goal; however, learning to be the right member of a local congregation might be even more challenging, and a critical responsibility all of us should face. In an excellent postcollege discipleship book, *Following Jesus in the "Real World,"* Richard Lamb emphasizes that we belong to a church in a meaningful way when we become a participant (not a mere consumer), a member (not a mere attender) and a partner (not a mere critic). For us Asian American young adults, I want to suggest, our becoming participants-members-partners in our churches is even more critical and challenging.

First, we need to recognize that the transition from our college Christian fellowship to a local church in the real world is quite difficult for many of us. Partly this difficulty is caused by the distorted images of churches that still haunt us. Another reason might be that, for some of us, our college fellowship ministry offered us for the very first time an experience of being participants-members-partners in a Christian community. We are wondering if we can find such a setting again in a local church.

The transition between a fellowship and the local church is challenging also because we ourselves are overwhelmed by many developments outside our church lives. Many of us will start a new job, or will be continually looking for a decent job or a better job. While struggling to pay our bills (including our huge education loans), we are wondering what our vocational calling is. Some of us are struggling with our relationship with our parents as we enter into a new phase of our lives. As they pressure us to go to grad schools or to get married to so-and-so, we wonder when we become an individuated, mature adult in the eyes of our parents. More fundamentally, many of us are trying to figure out "who I am" and "what I should do." With all these demands and pressures, we eventually feel emotionally spent and spiritually dry. The thought of taking a break from church life seems especially tempting during this period.

Belonging to a church is an essential ingredient in every Christian's discipleship. For Asian American young adults, however, active participation in church brings other particular benefits as well—including significant help with our identity formation. One scholar has observed that while Western culture says, "I think, therefore I am," the Asian culture declares, "I belong, therefore I am." In my Korean community, for example, I am not known as Peter (an autonomous individual) but as the late Pastor Cha's firstborn son (a member of a corporate group).

We come from a culture that places more emphasis on our last names than on our first names, that often places group identity above the individual one. Although we are Americanized, our Asian values have influenced us to define our identities also in terms of belonging to certain groups. To a varying degree one's understanding of "who I am" derives from what groups one belongs to. Indeed, some recent research points out that Asian American young people form their identities not in the context of individuation and separation but in the context of relationships and intimacy. In short, for Asian American young adults, belonging to a nurturing community in which one can find intimate and affirming relationships is particularly crucial—for it helps us to understand not only the spiritual identity of who we are in Christ but also our self-identity, or who we are as individuals.

If we understand the church to be the family of God, as the Bible teaches, then our ultimate goal cannot be simply to visit or explore different churches. After a period of prayerful search, we need to belong to a church, just as we belong to a family. We need to be willing to go through both good and rough times with a given family of God. Not too long ago, during one of my sermons, I shared with the congregation my desire to grow old together with them. One sister in the church came to me later and said how surprised she was to hear my expressed desire. While growing up she and her family moved from one church to another rather frequently, and she said that she was unconsciously thinking about staying at our church for about two years before moving on to another church. To her the thought of belonging to the same church for a significant period of time was a very novel concept.

At the same time, we are not called by our God to stay in one church throughout our lifetime. Sometimes God calls us out of one church even when we feel quite comfortable and content there. Sometimes we feel compelled to seek out a new church home when the church is moving in a direction that would call for us to compromise certain convictions that are important to us. Whatever the reason might be, transferring membership from one church to another should be a prayerful and thoughtful process. Are you thinking of leaving your current church for principled reasons? Are you not running away from something that you should confront or to which you should submit? Are you willing to leave your current church in a way that will minimize disturbance in the church? Is the new church a place that will stretch you to grow in those areas in which you have not seen much growth? Will the new church help you to participate in church life more fully? Will it stretch your kingdom vision?

Praying for the Health of Our Churches

Asian immigrant churches and Asian American churches are facing a great challenge. As mentioned earlier, 97 percent of Asian Americans are currently unchurched, making them one of the most unchurched people groups on this continent. How can we effectively reach out to our brothers and sisters? How can we stop the silent exodus of our young people from our churches?

My campus ministry experiences with Asian American fellowship groups remind me that many unchurched Asian Americans are spiritually receptive and that they desire to belong to a loving community. To use the language of our Savior Jesus, the harvest is ready. I do believe that our churches can become channels of God's saving grace when they grow as healthy congregations. The message of the gospel is ultimately an invitation to come and join the family of God and to grow together in his grace and love. This is a powerfully inviting message to our unchurched Asian American friends who are yearning to belong. For many of our previously churched friends who do understand this message of the gospel, they yearn to see this gospel in action, to witness the church living out its family life full of joy, love and health. God is calling our churches to grow as healthy congregations. God is calling each of us prayerfully to do our part in contributing to a healthy church life, no matter what kind of church we choose to be part of. Will you seriously consider this challenge?

11

Gifts Asian Americans Bring

Paul Tokunaga

I DON'T LIKE PARTIES MUCH, ESPECIALLY BIG ONES. FOR ME, MORE THAN six people is a crowd. This one was much bigger. I especially feel uncomfortable when I don't know most everyone. I'm not sure what to say or how to act. So when I got the invitation, I hesitated about going. But I knew the hosts. I liked them and I knew they would want me to come. I RSVP'd that I would be there.

I took along a little something, a small gift, as I always do when I visit someone's house. It's how I was brought up.

When I walked through the front door, I was stunned. Everyone was very well-dressed . . . tuxes, furs, heels, the whole deal. I had on my best, too, but I don't own much and I tend to be pretty casual anyway. I was tempted to slip back out the front door.

"You made it! I'm so glad you came! I was hoping you would."

She had always been a gracious hostess. It was almost like she didn't notice what I had on. I relaxed a bit.

The party went on. At some point toward the end, the host hollered out, "Let's all gather in the great room!"

As I walked in, I was again stunned—and dismayed. In the middle of the great room was a large table, the kind you would use for a banquet. On the table were large gifts. Large gifts. Most were ornately wrapped, like they probably do for you at Lord & Taylor's or Saks Fifth Avenue. I wouldn't know. I had brought something very small, very ordinary to me. I didn't know it was a gift-giving party. I kept it in my pocket. I slowly back-pedaled until I was leaning against the rear wall, trying to blend into it as best I could.

One by one, the host and hostess opened each gift. What great stuff! Stuff I wish I had, truth to tell. With the opening of each gift, our hosts lavished thanks on the giver. After seeing about ten of them opened, I made up my mind: no way was I going to put mine on that table. I would try to slip out. Later I would send a gift similar to the ones on that table, if I could afford it. Perhaps the hosts would forget I came and wouldn't realize I didn't leave a gift.

"Friends, this is all great. We love what you have brought us. They definitely are things we need, and we'll use them well. You were so kind."

That was my cue to slip out quietly.

"But it seems like one gift is, uhhh . . . missing. It was something we were kind of expecting from one of you. Did anyone see a gift that didn't get opened?"

In a panic, I looked around the room. No one was coming forward with a gift. And then, clearly, the host glanced at me.

I can't do this, *I thought.* My gift is so small and plain. I wrapped it myself. I'll be so embarrassed if I bring it up and they open it in front of everyone! They'll all laugh! I can't . . .

Then the hostess looked directly at me and smiled. I took a step, hesitated, drew in a deep breath and walked forward, head down, eyes on the floor. When I reached the table, I couldn't look up. I held out the gift. The wrapping was nearly coming off, having been squashed in my pocket all evening. More embarrassment.

"Ahhh . . ." said the host, his eyes sparkling.

"I wish I could have brought something else," was all I could get out.

As they opened it, an incredible thing happened. As the guests saw what I brought, ooohs and ahhhs enveloped the entire room. Then came loud clapping and cheering, even a few whistles, like at a football game. They were celebrating my little gift!

The host's eyes were getting moist. "It's exactly what we need."

The rest of the party was much better for me. Several people—important people—came up and commented on what a terrific gift I had brought. A few others just squeezed my shoulder as they walked by.

As the party ended, the hosts stood by the door, thanking each person for coming and for their gift. When I reached them, both of them reached out to me and embraced me. "It wouldn't have been complete without your gift. Thanks so much for bringing it."

I walked—actually sort of waltzed—into the crisp evening air. If only I had known it would mean that much to them. I would have given it to them much sooner.

We Belong!

The Bible is replete with parties and banquets. These gatherings of celebration inspired the party just described. In Isaiah 60 God foretells of a great gathering of diverse people groups coming together, each bringing gifts and offerings distinctive to their place and people. Jesus gives one picture of the future kingdom as he tells a parable of a wedding banquet in Matthew 22 and Luke 14.

The Bible also speaks clearly and often about each of us having a unique contribution to make in the kingdom. Paul uses the analogy of body parts in 1 Corinthians 12 to illustrate that a toe is not a hand, which is not an eye. Everyone brings something different, and all parts are needed for the body to function well.

Asian Americans have gifts to bring to the party. Our gifts are important as well as unique. We have some gifts that no one else can bring. Paul couldn't be clearer: "If the whole body were an eye, where would the hearing be? If the whole body were hearing, where would the sense of smell be?" (1 Corinthians 12:17).

Just As He Wanted Us to Be

Sometimes, if we are honest, we Asian Americans wonder if God made a mistake when he created us. It is not easy being a minority person. We are always comparing ourselves—consciously and subconsciously—with the majority culture. Do I measure up? Am I as good?

Do I have as much to offer? But hear the gospel: "God arranged the members in the body, *each one of them, as he chose*" (1 Corinthians 12:18). There was no celestial computer error when you were created Asian American. God didn't say, "Whoops! Darn! I meant Hon Eng to be Hans English! I meant Joe Ho to be Joe Holmes, but I forgot to finish his name!" He created us just the way he wanted. He wanted us Asian American.

God has not given us the freedom to question our worth in his body. To question our worth or place is to question his wisdom in creation. "The eye cannot say to the hand, 'I have no need of you' " (1 Corinthians 12:21). We may feel that sometimes the gift we bring is not worthy or does not measure up to the gifts of others, but that is never God's viewpoint. He wants what we have to bring. "On the contrary," continues Paul, "the members of the body that seem to be weaker are indispensable, and those members of the body that we think less honorable we clothe with greater honor" (1 Corinthians 12:22-23).

Here's a blunt interpretation of that verse for Asian Americans:

God doesn't make junk. You are loved by him just as much as the white person in the fellowship who seems to have it all together as an up-front leader. He loves you as much as the black person who can worship his socks off. Quit wasting so much energy comparing yourself and getting down for how you don't measure up. God gave you a whole lot and expects you to do something special with it. Leave your comfort zone, your only-if-I-were-like-so-and-so pity party, and be a working part of the body. Get in the game!

Thankfully, God is no cookie-cutter creator. Each person, as well as each culture, is unique. Culture is not "gospel-neutral." We must always examine our culture in the light of God's word. As we do that, it will be clear that there are some aspects that are consistent with the Christian faith and some that work against it.

There are some wonderful aspects of being Asian American that give us special contributions to make to the kingdom. These contributions are not better (or worse) than the contributions of any other culture. Indeed, people of other ethnicities have some of these qualities, but they seem to be consistently present in many Asian American

Christians. Whether you are in a church or fellowship that is all-Asian American or one that is multiethnic, here are five unique gifts Asian Americans bring to the kingdom of God: deep friendships and being the community glue, hospitality evangelism, bridge people for racial healing, our wealth and education, and our pain.

Deep Friendships and Being the Community Glue

People are starving for a really good friend. Everyone is yearning for a "friend of the soul," someone who understands them at a deep level. Each of us needs one or two people with whom there are no secrets and no games are played. We all want to know intimately and to be known intimately. Unfortunately, rarely do we actually experience this.

Few of us are very good at making deep friendships. Current American culture is ragged with distrust toward others. *What does he want from me? What are her motives? What will happen if I let my guard down and let the real me come out?* America's eroding family life has lost a foundation of trust and security that is still found in most Asian families.

Asian Americans are strong in developing trusting friendships. We have qualities that quietly shout out to others, "I can be a good friend!" Perhaps thanks to our Confucian heritage, we know how to care for others, are good listeners and are trustworthy and dependable. We tend to feel deeply what others feel. We know how to walk in their shoes. Once others get to know us (which is frequently the hardest part), they often can't get enough of us.

Takie Sugiyama Lebra, in *Japanese Patterns of Behavior,* writes:

For the Japanese, empathy (or omoiyari) ranks high among the virtues considered indispensable for one to be really human, morally mature, and deserving of respect. I am even tempted to call Japanese culture an omoiyari culture . . . Omoiyari refers to the ability and willingness to feel what others are feeling, to vicariously experience the pleasure or pain that they are undergoing, and to help them satisfy their wishes. . . .

While omoiyari is characteristic in Japanese people, it also exists in other Asian cultures.

A huge gift we can give to the kingdom of God is developing a deep friendship with a non-Asian American Christian. Not only will that person never be quite the same again, but we will be changed as well. We will be stretched and challenged to have a deep friendship with someone who is ethnically very different from us.

One of the strong qualities of this generation is the desire to be in community. That desire, however, often runs ahead of the ability to be a healthy, functioning community. What you find in many churches and fellowships is the dangerous mix of strong Western individualism and a deep need for acceptance and security. Clearly an ingredient is missing. Often it's a good portion of Asian Americans. Omoiyari people are very communal and loyal by nature. For any community to function well, it needs some omoiyari people.

> ## Omoiyari People
>
> Lebra says, "Omoiyari people seek to maintain consensus or agreement by deferring to the fulfillment of each other's needs and desires. They also seek to optimize each other's comfort by seeking to provide pleasure or prevent displeasure by anticipating the other's needs and desires and taking initiative to meet those needs and fulfill them without the other person having to overtly express them in some obvious way." (Japanese Patterns of Behavior)

When I served as staff member for the InterVarsity fellowship at Florida State University, one of the members of the leadership team was June Inouye, a Japanese American and the only Asian American in a group of about seventy-five. Perhaps the quietest member, June was always two steps ahead of others in anticipating the needs of the fellowship, especially the leadership team. She was the glue the community needed. Over the years my wife, Margaret, and I have become good friends with June's parents, Denis and Toshiko. We have been guests in their home and enjoyed their gracious hospitality. It is clear where June learned omoiyari. We have always felt "looked out for" in their home.

Before we pat ourselves too hard on the back, however, we also need to hear our critics. Asian Americans are too reserved . . . they're too passive . . . they're always avoiding conflicts. They're not the easiest people with whom to develop deep relationships. Where that is indeed true, let's own it, repent and work on developing better relational patterns.

Hospitality Evangelism
Bring up evangelism with Asian Americans and it's often a pretty short discussion. Asian Americans generally are not strong in reaching unchurched nonbelievers. We don't like evangelism because it feels too confrontational, something we avoid at all costs. We don't like to put people on the spot. Ambiguity is more comfortable.

But evangelism is important. Evangelism is the difference between eternal life and death. We have too many nonbelieving friends and family members on their way to hell for us to say, "Evangelism is not for me. Leave it to the extroverted white folks." I believe fruitful evangelism in the next decade will almost exclusively be done in the context of trusting friendships. The hunger to have a friend of the soul is often the best doorway to asking questions *about* the soul.

Hand in hand with being able to make trusting friendships is the ability to offer gracious hospitality. Think of the last time you were in the home of an Asian American friend or relative. From the moment you were greeted at the door (and slipped your shoes off) and were offered delicious refreshments in a comfortable setting, you knew you were in a *home.*

I went to college in the town where my Auntie Shizuko lived. She is a *kibbei,* born in the United States, sent to Japan to be educated and then returned to the States. Whenever I needed to escape dorm life and cafeteria food my freshman year, I would drop in on Auntie. She would treat me like a weary scholar needing a respite from the harsh demands of academia. (Yes, I would tell her, Organic Gardening 101 is awfully difficult.) I would plop down on her comfy sofa, pet one of her several cats and sip the cold drink she had just handed me.

My dorm pals Mark and Dave would sometimes hint for a dinner invitation to Auntie's. Once she served us a huge tray of enchiladas, a splendid dinner that we vacuumed from the table in five minutes. Then we sniffed something wonderful sizzling on the stove. We looked at each other, "Nah, can't be." Being cafeteria connoisseurs, we had all but forgotten the smell of steak. Sure enough, Auntie Shizuko brought out the main course—three massive sirloin steaks! When we asked her to join us, she politely refused. She preferred to stay in the kitchen and cook for us.

I have been in enough Asian American homes to know it is not just Auntie Shizuko. My friends have often said the same thing. "It's so warm at Kyung's place." "Steve makes you feel special." "Sumi works so hard to throw a great dinner party." In my own family, relatives on Mom's side gather every Thanksgiving at our house. One of her golfing buddies comes each year and for a day becomes one of the Tokunagas. I'm sure Mom's ability to make her feel like one of the family is a big part of it.

Our gifts in hospitality are a perfect partner for evangelism. We invite Christians into our homes regularly; why not do the same kinds of things with non-Christians? I am not making a case here for formal evangelistic supper parties, which may have their place. Simply, as we have non-Christians in our homes (just as we have Christians in), we will provide a warm, natural setting to talk about things of the heart and soul.

Sitting, standing, walking and playing all around us are nonbelievers looking for genuine people who stand for something important—and care about them. If we could be mentored by non-Asians who are experienced in the evangelism side of friendship evangelism, I'm convinced we could become very good evangelists.

Bridge People for Racial Healing

Contemporary writers within and outside of Christendom believe America is on the verge of race wars. This is no melting pot, and hardly the village that Hillary Rodham Clinton envisions. Instead, we are seeing the "balkanization" of America. We are dividing up into ethnic groups more than ever. Lines are drawn thicker every day, walls are going higher. Many of them are lined with barbed wire and "Stay Out" signs.

It's not just a black-white thing. It's a black-Korean thing. It's a white-Hispanic thing. Different Asian nationalities with sordid and morbid histories still don't fully trust each other. (Ever wonder why there aren't more Japanese-and-Korean churches?)

Racism is not just a problem for the politicos to wrangle over and solve. It is a deeply spiritual problem that can only be tamed by spiritual solutions. Reconciliation—including the racial variety—is at the gospel's heart. We can't ignore it. We can't hide from it. By exercising "ostrich theology"—sticking our heads in the ground—we are making things worse. We are telling the world that Christians don't care. That is not right.

I believe Asian American Christians are specially poised in our history to play a key role in the worst racial divide in our country, the one between blacks and whites. Asian Americans have gained some trust and respect from both blacks and whites. (Granted, Korean Americans and African Americans have conflicts to resolve.) Just as Jimmy Carter has been a tremendous third-party mediator between warring nations, might Asian American Christians be the needed Jimmy Carters, bridging the gap between blacks and whites?

Our son, Sam, is in the seventh grade at a magnet school mandated by the U.S. Supreme Court as part of the desegregation process for public schools in our county in Atlanta. The makeup of the student body is 50 percent African American and 50 percent everyone else. For his social science project this year, Sam decided to tackle a controversial but important issue at his school: how racist are the students in his grade? He put together a survey that was taken by all seventh graders. One of his (milder) questions was "Why do blacks and whites eat at separate tables in the cafeteria?"

As we drove to the bus stop recently, I asked him, "Where do you sit, Sam?"

"Sometimes I sit at the white tables and sometimes I sit at the black tables."

I asked him if any of the other kids ate with those of a different color. "Only On [another Asian American] and me," was his reply.

Sam just celebrated his thirteenth birthday. We did it up big. We told him he could invite eleven friends to an athletic facility that had batting cages, full-court basketball, whiffle ball—birthday heaven for seventh-grade boys. When he gave us his list, I was pleased but not too surprised. On it were the names of six African Americans, one Asian immigrant and four Caucasians. Of course, I had to ask him, "If any of your friends from school were throwing a party like this, would their list look like yours?"

"Nope," he answered. "They'd be almost all black or almost all white."

Slowly, Sam, who is half Asian American and half Caucasian, is beginning to understand a unique role he can play as a "bridge person" between blacks and whites.

My wife, Margaret, grew up in a very segregated Mississippi from the fifties through the early seventies. She says she lived in fear of blacks and in ignorance of their world. When we had Sam, she said, "I will not raise a son who fears blacks and doesn't have a clue as to what their world is like." Intentionally we have lived in mixed neighborhoods and put Sam in mixed public schools and extracurricular programs. When Sam chose the topic for his project, Margaret felt a sense of redemption for her past.

Being a bridge person between blacks and whites or bringing reconciliation between fellow Asian Americans or between Caucasians and Asian Americans is an enormous task. It takes time and energy. It is usually incredibly slow, drawn out and complex beyond belief. Most of us probably are not called to racial reconciliation on that level, though some of us are. All of us who are Asian American Christians can do something, though. Each of us is capable of having a good friendship with a person of another color. We have much to offer and much to gain. It will mean breaking out of the comfort zones of who we naturally spend time with. Each of us is confronted regularly with attitudes and conduct that "just aren't right." Prayerfully, we can choose which of these we can oppose and then stand up for what is right. Each of us has prejudices to overcome. We can be diligent in working on these in the context of a like-minded community of faith.

Our Wealth and Education

Per capita, Asian Americans have the second highest income in America. Our median income is roughly $6,000 more than the American average. For those of us who have given our lives to Jesus Christ, we know that the wealth we may possess is not ours. We mouth that "this is God's money and I am to be a good steward of it." However, Asian Americans like to have the best, if they can afford it. Asian American Christians aren't often much different than their nonbelieving Asian American friends. Our homes, cars and wardrobes look pretty similar.

As Asian Americans enter third, fourth and fifth generations, we have growing freedom to become missionaries and Christian workers. With the explosion of parachurch ministries, options abound. Most options involve raising one's support to cover salary and ministry expenses. This is where fellow Asian American Christians can play a strategic role.

If we say that our wealth is from God and the money belongs to him and is on loan to us to use wisely, then let's do so. Do I really need that new Lexus, or would a used Honda serve me just as well? Do I really have to live in that exclusive suburb, or could my family do just as well in one a few notches lower on the subdivision chain? With a few different lifestyle choices, how much money could we free up for God's work?

Some of us are still college students; wealth is not yet an issue. Our current wealth might be our intellect and our education. For all Asian Americans, 49 percent have college degrees, compared with 28 percent for the U.S. population in general. Tacky stereotypes aside, Japanese Americans, Korean Americans and Chinese Americans on the whole are a pretty smart lot. We may not be Asian whiz kids in math and science, but a lot of us do pretty well in other areas. We also do pretty well at some pretty decent schools. Our parents' sacrifices have not been in vain.

Now, not ten years after we graduate, is the time to start asking some candid "stewardship of our talents" questions. "If God truly gave me this mind and my parents gave me the opportunity to get a first-rate education, how can I be the best steward of it?" If we wait ten years, we will be knee-deep in quarter-million dollar mortgages and twenty-five-thousand-dollar cars to pay for, and the voice of God will be muted and faint, if not completely drowned out.

"How can I use my intellectual gifts and a great education to glorify God and help others?" If we can muster the courage to ask that question, the possibilities will be endless.

Yesterday I had a Coke with Patrick, a twentysomething in the Chinese church we attend. Patrick majored in industrial engineering at Georgia Tech and is currently working as a consultant. He and a few other young men from the church have a dream: in a few years, they leave their jobs, form a company and manufacture a product. Here's the ingenious part: they make enough money that, on a rotating basis, one or two of the five-person leadership team can do missionary work for several years, funded by the company. With a twinkle in his eye, he asks, "Want to join us?"

The Gift of Pain

That is not a typographical error.

Asian American young people are in lots of pain these days. As this book has amply revealed, there is immense pain brought about by our relationships with our parents. But not all of our pain comes from home. Some of it comes from the tension of being bicultural people. Living with one foot in our Asian world and the other in America is not easy. These are two very different worlds. Our pain has still other sources: the pressures we put on ourselves (chapter one) and gender pressures (chapter seven) are just two of them.

Pain hurts, but pain also can be a gift. When we are able to see the tough times as part of God's way to shape, restore and refinish us, the pain they produce has a redemptive by-product. Does it relieve the pain? Nope. Does it help us to experience it differently? It can.

I am now able to look back at a pretty difficult adolescence through different lenses. Yes, those painful experiences still took place. But time and God have given me some different ways of viewing them. For example, as Mom and Dad were the perennial bad guys, I can now see how I was a pretty hard kid to raise. As a result, when I talk with a younger person in the middle of an extremely tough family situation, I can walk through it with him or her with some understanding. My personal pain becomes a healing balm for another.

Working on this book with the other writers was a wonderful gift from God. We met twice to work together for several days. As we discussed each chapter, we told story after story. I felt like I was on the set of a Christian *Joy Luck Club*. Often we laughed at each other's stories; sometimes we cried. As Jeanette, Greg, Peter and Susan shared their pain, I was healed of my some of my own pain. Our stories, though unique, were often so similar.

Do only Asian Americans suffer and experience pain? Certainly not! But with Asian Americans, there is a unique mix of pain and "omoiyariness," the ability to deeply empathize with others, that gives us something distinctive to offer others in pain. You will never live painlessly. Scripture makes that clear. However, you can use your pain redemptively as a gift to share with others.

What Keeps Us from Bringing Our Gifts?

In "Following Jesus as an Asian American," Tom Lin identifies several barriers in Asian American culture that keep us from being full participants in the body of Christ, including:

☐ *Low self-esteem.* According to Iwa Ministries and other demographic surveys, Asian Americans continue to have the lowest self-esteem of any demographic group in America.

☐ *Drivenness and emphasis on security.* This stems from the influence of the immigrant culture, where financial security did not come easily. To slow down the rat race and put our security in Jesus is very difficult and often too big a step for Asian Americans to take.

☐ *Ethnocentrism* (even between specific Asian groups). At an international student gathering in 1994, a large Japanese delegation knelt to the floor and asked forgiveness of the Korean delegation. The Japanese Christians chose to identify with the sins their ancestors had committed against Koreans, bringing about reconciliation, and to put to an end the old hostility between the two cultures. Today, ethnocentrism remains in many Asian American homes and upbringings (*Diversity and Distinction: Celebrating Uniqueness at Harvard,* 1, no. 2 [1995]).

I would add three other temptations we face to keep our gifts to ourselves:

☐ *Prejudice and racism* (close cousins to ethnocentrism). Not only do we like our own, we also don't like some of the others who join us at the table. White people can intimidate us, black people can scare us, and some Hispanic people are below our dignity. These are not nice things to say, but they are often too true of us.

Our comfort zone is rather small and defined. We have room for only certain types of people. African-Americans are too loud and demonstrative. White folks are too straightforward. Hispanic Americans can't be trusted.

Even with our own, we put up walls. As a child, I sensed a pecking order. Japanese Americans, of course, were on the top, followed by Chinese Americans (not a close second), with Filipino Americans a distant third. We didn't know any Korean Americans, so they weren't ranked. All of us have our own private rankings.

☐ *Timidity and conformity.* Perhaps byproducts of low self-esteem, they infect many Asian Americans. Our timidity holds us back from all that we have to offer. We may couch it in phrases like these: "I'm Asian," "I prefer to be indirect," "I don't like to make waves," "I don't like to be up front and in the limelight," or "Can't I just bring refreshments?" The result is that the body of Christ is robbed of the great things we have to give, and we are frustrated that we aren't fully appreciated for what we know we have to offer.

Conformity is best expressed in an Asian proverb: the nail that sticks up gets pounded down. When a minority group is trying to establish itself in a new country, blending in usually works better than making a scene. Conformity and values such as risking all for Jesus, standing up for your faith, and being a radical Christian don't usually blend in too well. How many open-air Asian American evangelists have shown up on campus recently?

☐ *Gender stereotypes.* Asian women shouldn't lead. They should just be behind the scenes. They should always take their cues from the men.

Asian men are not expressive and vulnerable. They aren't intimate. They are geeks. It can be hard to break through and act differently than expected.

Being Available

It is fine to acknowledge such possible temptations, but probably it is not helpful to dwell on them. It is too easy to excuse ourselves from living like and being like Jesus. Rather, we ought to ask the Lord, "How have you gifted me? What passions do I have? What people in my world need what I have to offer?"

When I was a sophomore at Cal Poly-San Luis Obispo, God slowly put a love in my heart for my campus. More than anything, I wanted to see the entire campus wrestle with the greatness of Jesus Christ. He was dramatically changing my life, and I couldn't keep it to myself. I started asking God, "How can I love Cal Poly?" This may not have been the smartest question for a fairly new believer who was struggling with low self-esteem, ethnic identity, thick glasses, acne and pudginess, but God had gotten hold of me in a powerful, undeniable way. I felt like David when he said, "I cannot be silent." "You turned my wailing into dancing; you removed my sackcloth and clothed me with joy, that my heart may sing to you and not be silent" (Ps 30:11-12 NIV).

I shared my faith: in the classroom . . . with my roommate . . . down the hall. A friend who was discipling me took me to parties with her old druggie friends. We shared Jesus with them. We walked the streets of San Luis Obispo at night and told strangers how to find God.

Personal evangelism was great, but I sensed there was more to following Jesus. "What else, God?"

I joined InterVarsity Christian Fellowship. There was a huge new dorm on campus, Yosemite Hall, without a witness for Jesus. Gary and I started a small group Bible study there. I started writing for the *Mustang Daily,* the school paper. As I became a trusted writer and editor, I was given tremendous freedom to report on Christian activities and testify about the work God was doing in fellow students' lives.

I was a student during violent times on many California campuses. I made a commitment to nonviolence and protecting my campus from violent campus riots. I met with the college president and pledged my support. On the brink of a potential riot, he chose to call on our fellowship rather than the National Guard to protect his campus. I put together a plan to blockade demonstrators so that they couldn't destroy parts of the campus, if that came to pass. At one very scary point, I muttered a prayer: "Lord, pudgy Japanese Americans with acne and thick glasses don't usually do this sort of thing, but if you are in this—count me in!"

During my junior year I asked again, "What else, God?" I ran for student body president on a Christ-centered platform with two Christian leaders in the fellowship. This was not a great way for an introvert to spend a pretty California spring. I was speaking at rallies, doing debates, getting heckled by Jesus-haters and meeting hundreds of strangers. Stepping—no, leaping—out of my comfort zone was both exhilarating and exhausting. Getting a tan on the beach with one or two friends was usually how I spent my free time in the spring.

The result? I got clobbered by my two opponents. In Asian lingo, we might say I had achieved the trifecta of losing face and being publicly shamed and humiliated. But God's agenda goes beyond our discomfort.

During the campaign the eventual winner told me he wanted Jesus in his life, and I had the honor of leading him to Christ. I spent my senior year discipling the student body president, spending every weekday morning in Bible study and prayer for the campus.

Someone clever once said, "God wants our availability more than he wants our ability." That may be theologically sound, but why not give him both? What could sound sweeter to God than "I'm available, Lord. What can you do with what I bring?"

* * *

"It's exactly what we need," was his answer.

As they opened it, an incredible thing happened. As the guests saw what I brought, ooohs and ahhhs enveloped the entire room. Then came loud clapping and cheering, even a few whistles, like at a football game. They were celebrating my little gift!

The host's eyes were getting moist. "It's exactly what we need."

The rest of the party was much better for me. Several people—important people—came up and commented on what a terrific gift I had brought. A few others just squeezed my shoulder as they walked by.

As the party ended, the hosts stood by the door, thanking each person for coming and for their gift. When I reached them, both of them reached out to me and embraced me. "It wouldn't have been complete without your gift. Thanks so much for bringing it."

I walked—actually sort of waltzed—into the crisp evening air. If only I had known it would mean that much to them. I would have given it to them much sooner.

For Further Reading

Personal Identity

Lin, Tom. *Losing Face and Finding Grace: 12 Bible Studies for Asian-Americans.* Downers Grove, Ill.: InterVarsity Press, 1995.

Family

Clapp, Rodney. *Families at the Crossroads: Beyond Traditional & Modern Options.* Downers Grove, Ill.: InterVarsity Press, 1993.

Guest, Joan. *Forgiving Your Parents.* Downers Grove, Ill.: InterVarsity Press, 1988.

Spiritual Life

Blue, Ken. *Healing Spiritual Abuse.* Downers Grove, Ill.: InterVarsity Press, 1993.

Grenz, Stanley J., and Denise Muir Kjesbo. *Women in the Church.* Downers Grove, Ill.: InterVarsity Press, 1995.

Lamb, Richard. *Following Jesus in the "Real World": Discipleship for the Post-College Years.* Downers Grove, Ill.: InterVarsity Press, 1995.

Manning, Brennan. *The Ragamuffin Gospel.* Portland, Ore.: Multnomah Press, 1990.

Mickelsen, Alvera, ed. *Women, Authority & the Bible.* Downers Grove, Ill.: InterVarsity Press, 1986.

Nouwen, Henri J. M. *The Wounded Healer.* Garden City, N.Y.: Doubleday, 1972.

———. *The Return of the Prodigal Son.* New York: Image Books, 1992.

Peterson, Eugene. *A Long Obedience in the Same Direction.* Downers Grove, Ill.: InterVarsity Press, 1980.

Smith, Gordon T. *Listening to God in Times of Choice.* Downers Grove, Ill.: InterVarsity Press, 1997.

White, John. *The Fight.* Downers Grove, Ill.: InterVarsity Press, 1978.

Asian American and Asian History

Kitano, Harry H. L., and Roger Daniels. *Asian Americans, Emerging Minorities.* Englewood Cliffs, N.J.: Prentice-Hall, 1988.

Lee, Joann Faung Jean. *Asian Americans.* New York: New Press, 1992.

Moffett, Samuel Hugh. *A History of Christianity in Asia.* 2 vols. San Francisco: HarperCollins, 1992-1997.

Takaki, Ronald. *Strangers from a Different Shore,* Boston: Little, Brown, 1989.

Ethnic and Crosscultural Issues

Hong, Maria, ed. *Growing Up Asian American: An Anthology.* New York: Wm. Morrow, 1993.

Karnow, Stanley, and Nancy Yoshihara. *Asian Americans in Transition.* New York: Asia Society, 1992.

Lee, Mary Paik. *Quiet Odyssey: A Pioneer Korean Woman in America.* Seattle: University of Washington Press, 1990.

Ligenfelter, Sherwood G., and Marvin Mayers. *Ministering Cross-Culturally.* Grand Rapids, Mich.: Baker, 1996.

Park, Andrew Sung. *Racial Conflict & Healing: An Asian-American Theological Perspective.* Maryknoll, N.Y.: Orbis Books, 1996.

Perkins, John. *Let Justice Roll Down.* Glendale, Calif.: Regal Books, 1976.

———. *With Justice for All.* Ventura, Calif.: Regal Books, 1982.

Perkins, Spencer, and Chris Rice. *More Than Equals.* Downers Grove, Ill.: InterVarsity Press, 1993.

Slater, Philip. *The Pursuit of Loneliness: American Culture at the Breaking Point.* Boston: Beacon, 1990.

Tan, Amy. *The Joy Luck Club.* New York: Putnam's, 1989.

Tuan-MacLean, Katherine. "The Interracial Friendships of White and Asian College Students." Ph.D. dissertation, Northwestern University, 1996.

Contributors

Jeanette Yep, an American-born Chinese, served as the coordinator of this project. Jeanette was an InterVarsity Christian Fellowship student leader at Mount Holyoke College. After graduation she spent a year studying Chinese language and culture in Taiwan. Recently she received a master's degree in communications from Northwestern University. Now in her twenty-first year on IV staff, she is a divisional director, based in Chicago. She is affectionately known by Urbana delegates as "Auntie Jeanette."

Peter Cha is a 1.5 generation Korean pastor of Parkwood Community Church, an Asian American church serving Chicagoland. He served on InterVarsity staff for ten years. At Trinity Evangelical Divinity School, where he earned his M.Div., Peter teaches practical theology courses, specializing in ethnic and cultural issues. In his spare time Peter is completing his Ph.D. at Northwestern University. He and his wife, Phyllis, are the proud parents of Nathaniel and Elaine.

Susan Cho Van Riesen's parents immigrated from Korea when she was five. Susan is a graduate of Occidental College in Los Angeles, where she is now an InterVarsity staff worker. Susan worked on this project during busy months of planning her marriage to Alex Van Riesen and completed revisions after her honeymoon.

Greg Jao is an American-born Chinese. He is a campus staff worker with InterVarsity at his alma mater, the University of Chicago. He holds a law degree from Northwestern Law School and assists in the legal department of InterVarsity. Most of Greg's expendable income goes to his extensive book collection (for which InterVarsity Press is grateful).

Paul Tokunaga is a Sansei (third generation Japanese American). He is the national coordinator of Asian American Ministries for InterVarsity Christian Fellowship. He started with InterVarsity as a student at Cal Poly and has also worked with 2100 Productions and as Southeast Regional Director. He has a master's degree in Christian Studies from New College, Berkeley. Paul and his wife, Margaret, live in Atlanta, Georgia, where he collects baseball cards with his son, Sam.

Collectively, the team represents eighty years of student ministry experience!